Praise For The Family Altar

I have watched Pastor Karolina's journey for more than twenty years - in her role as leader and pastor, as a mother, and as a wife. I have seen her navigate the tension between her personal life and her public life. I have witnessed her endure the most tragic circumstances and watched her rebuild a beautiful future in both her family and her ministry.

What she offers in this book does not come merely from knowledge but from life experience—both victories and challenges. Her love for family and God, and her understanding of how these are the foundation of a better future, will inspire you and prepare you to see the best in your life, your family, and the world around you.

Mark Ramsey
Global Senior Pastor, Citipointe Church

+++

I have known Karolina for over twenty years, and she has always been a 'deep well'. I observed her journey through the furnace of affliction and emerge even deeper, in faith, character, and anointing.

Karolina is known as an exceptional church leader and communicator, but in this book, we encounter something more: her prophetic voice.

Many helpful books have been written for Christian parents, but this one is different. *The Family Altar* is a prophetic revelation of God's plan and purpose for families, and a call to come up higher. Yes, this book is practical and helpful, but it is more. Weighty, but not heavy, profound and accessible, *The Family Altar* will inspire and encourage you.

I pray you catch this revelation and are changed.

Vicki Simpson
Director, She's The Voice Inc.
Minister, C3 Church Global

+++

The Family Altar is a timely and prophetic book. Karolina has brought a beautiful and challenging reminder that with prayerfulness, conviction, and intentionality, we can ensure our families return to the divine plan that God intended for them. This isn't just a book filled with theories, but one that has been lovingly outworked in her own family, even through the fire of extraordinary challenges.

I've known Karolina for many years, and she doesn't just preach — she practices! Her life has always been about sowing seeds into the next generation, and this book continues to do that through the lens of family. It carries the power to bring about an awakening in our homes that will lead to impact across our world.

Jo Geerling
Senior Pastor, iSee Church

+++

I had the joy of meeting Karolina at a women's conference in Australia. The God-connection was immediate as we both leaned in and taught from our individual journeys - journeys that, while different, shared a common thread: the desire and choice to overcome the challenges that life inevitably presents.

I believe her book, *The Family Altar*, carries immense wisdom from a truly unique landscape and testimony. The God I know and love places great value upon family, and I am confident that this beautiful labour of love, from her life and her altar to yours, will yield immense blessing and fruit.

Bobbie Houston

Founder, Hillsong Church

+++

Karolina Grant has lived her love for Jesus and for people with grace and joy amid deep suffering. Her story weaves God's faithfulness throughout her journey, offering a beautiful tapestry of hope for every person. Whether you have suffered setbacks at home or are just looking to strengthen your family, I couldn't recommend this book more.

Anna R. Morgan, DIS, Fuller Theological Seminary

Lead Pastor, Word of Life.
V.P. Of Academics, Ascent College.
Assistant Professor of Leadership, Fuller Theological Seminary.

How beautifully Karolina's pen has captured the 'Sacred Place of God' for her wonderful family.

A place where words and touch are edifying and gentle. A place where hurting hearts can continue to beat in hope and healing. A place where each soul has equal value, and correction is offered with grace and wisdom. A place where each family member is heard, seen, and honoured. A place where Jesus Christ is always the centre of every relationship and conversation.

Having established, with my wife, a family altar around our dinner table, we have cherished the genuine close relationships our five adult children share with each other's families over the past three decades. Whenever we visit Karolina's home and family, it is delightful to experience her sacred altar with her husband Jared and their seven children.

This volume is not just a book on Christian family culture, but a tapestry of legacy, guiding children toward a functional and rewarding family life into eternity.

Dr Charles Gullo

MSc (ULond); BDSc (UQ); Adv Dip Theo & Min; FCHC

+++

I finished *The Family Altar* with tears in my eyes and a deep sense of holy expectation. This is not simply a well-written book - it is a timely and necessary one.

What struck me most is the clarity with which Karolina articulates God's unchanging design for humanity. As a mother of sons, I was deeply moved by the way Karolina restores dignity, purpose, and God-given calling to men and boys. As a woman, I was reminded of the strength and freedom found in embracing God's call on womanhood. And as a pastor, my heart is full of hope for the marriages and families who will encounter God's transforming work through these pages, and for the generational legacy that will follow.

I also write as a friend. I have watched Karolina live the truths she writes about - through seasons of joy and devastating loss, through grief, restoration, remarriage, and the forming of a blended family marked by God's grace. Through it all, she has remained anchored to God and His Word, and I have seen the fruit of that faith not only in her own life, but in her marriage, her children, her church, and her wider community.

This is a book that, if embraced and lived, has the power to reshape culture.

Rebecca Connett
Senior Pastor, Goodlife Church

+++

Karolina Grant is a mighty woman of God with an incredible story to tell. Her life carries a deep revelation of God's work in and through the family. From childhood, through the loss of her first husband, and now into the beautiful story of God's redemption and restoration, her lived experience of building an altar to the Lord in her home is one that will inspire many.

As I travel the world preaching the gospel and witnessing the ways the Lord is bringing revival and renewal to cities and nations, one thing is clear: in order for true reformation and transformation to take place, revival must permeate the family.

I believe *The Family Altar* is both a prophetic call and a practical blueprint for anyone who desires to partner with what the Lord is doing across the earth, bringing revival to and through families.

Layla Nahavandi
Founder, The Burning Hearts Movement

+++

The Family Altar is a timely and deeply biblical call to re-centre faith where it has always been meant to begin: in the home. In a world marked by hurry and hustle, Pastor Karolina Grant presents a compelling vision of households becoming places of worship, formation, and the presence of God for our children and our children's children.

I read this book not only as a pastor, but as someone raised in a home of six children by parents who were devoted followers of Jesus and faithful pastors. I have seen firsthand the formative power of a home where prayer, Scripture, and worship were lived daily. That legacy now shapes my own commitment to lead my wife, our three children, and our church community around the altar and the importance of biblical family values.

This book offers no formulas or perfectionism, but a gracious and courageous invitation to slow down and rebuild what truly matters. It will encourage parents, strengthen marriages, and remind church leaders that discipleship begins in the home.

Alex Tan
Senior Pastor, hm.church

+++

From honest and raw portraits of marriage, a focus on the heartbeat of family life, and the reminder of how the Sabbath is still so powerful, as is family worship, the author paints a beautiful picture of raising a generation anchored in faith.

In a culture that pulls families apart and encourages us to disconnect, this book does the opposite, calling us back to Christ-centred homes where love is practiced daily, and the home becomes the centre of nurture and connection. An encouraging and hope-filled read for any parent longing to build a family that still believes.

Kathy Abraham
Chair, International Network of Churches (INC)

+++

In today's ever-changing world, we often face devastation that threatens our hopes and futures. But amid this chaos, a profound truth emerges: while the spirit of this world seeks to pull us apart, the Spirit of God draws us together - restoring what has been lost and rebuilding futures once thought irretrievable.

Pastor Karolina has demonstrated that the power of unity and reconciliation far surpasses the forces that tear us apart. Loss may level the landscape, but faith breathes life into the unseen riches that lie ahead. God, our ultimate Creator, continually shapes new tomorrows, new journeys, and new destinies. The Holy Spirit empowers us with the resilience to love and laugh again.

Pastor Karolina's unwavering faith, bravery, and openness stand as living evidence that "all things are possible through Christ who strengthens me" (Philippians 4:13). I wholeheartedly commend Pastor Karolina's book, *The Family Altar*, to you. Her words of wisdom and profound insight are a precious gift, as she courageously opens her heart and invites you into her deeply personal world.

Bev Mortlock BA.Min

Founding Pastor, City Impact Churches International

THE FAMILY ALTAR

KAROLINA GRANT

Ark House Press
arkhousepress.com

Cataloguing in Publication Data:
Title: The Family Altar
ISBN: 978-1-7644430-6-7 (pbk)
Subjects: [REL012030] RELIGION / Christian Living / Family & Relationships; [REL012130] RELIGION / Christian Living / Women's Interests; [REL074000] RELIGION / Christian Ministry / Pastoral Resources.

Cover design by Jess Steer
Design by initiateagency.com

DEDICATION

To Sam Gunsser
and
Karen Grant.

Your legacy lives.

TABLE OF CONTENTS

THE FAMILY ALTAR

By Karolina Grant

At the time of writing, I'm 43 years old and have seven children between the ages of six and 19. Four of them I carried and gave birth to; three I welcomed into my heart when I married for a second time, after the passing of my first husband. Writing those words in reflection and summation of my reality continues to blow my mind. I can hardly believe the life I live.

Life has been full of unexpected surprises, both elation at its highest, and the devastating depths of despair, with the somewhat mundane and unassuming in-between. There's no way to predict either one of the extremes. They simply greet us and we must welcome them as guests, wanted or not.

My Polish immigrant family broke down when I was 12 years old. Life seemed to become significantly more difficult. Although I was confident of the love both my parents had for me, I was desperate for the security and the ideal of family. I was disappointed at my core, and wrestled with deep feelings of inferiority and abandonment. I often found myself meditating on the hopes that, maybe one day, I could build a home of my own, and that it would be different for me.

It was during this season of difficulty that my mother encountered Christ, and brought my sisters and I with her into a new Church community. I felt my soul begin to breathe. I felt hope rise in my heart. I felt darkness retreat, as the light of salvation shone brightly in my being. My pastors and my new friends modelled lives that I admired. I was beginning to dream.

I have loved the Lord since the age of 12, when my youth pastor led me to Christ in a camp dining hall during a Church family retreat. I would later rededicate my life to Christ at 18 years of age, after a season of wandering in the wilderness as a teenager.

That recommitment in the altar of a Church, as a very broken 18-year-old university student, changed the entire trajectory of my life. I walked through the narrow gate, and I found the narrow road. Jesus wasn't lying when He promised this was the path that would lead to life. I will always be grateful for His grace in allowing me to find it.

At the sweet age of 19, I was engaged to a young Christian man named Samuel Gunsser. He was honourable and servant-hearted. He was a leader among the young adults in this new Church I had found myself in. He was diligent, strong, generous, and kind. We had only been dating for four months when he asked me to be his wife, with a beautiful diamond ring which he purchased with the money he earned working three different jobs. I was surprised, but I was certain.

We were married when I was 20, and he was 25. Together we built a beautiful life. We were in ministry together, which was another surprise to me. I was shocked at the kindness of God; that He would choose me to be a minister of the Gospel, and that He would provide such an incredible husband and life for me. According to my evaluation, I should have been the last person to be the recipient of such graces. But I was a willing recipient all the same. I did everything I could to learn the things I didn't know. I committed myself to studying Christian literature on marriage, family, finance, leadership, mindsets, and the nature of God. To this day, my library is filled with titles under these themes.

Sam and I were married for 19 years. We were devoted to raising our children, and leading our Church family, when he was diagnosed with a disease that would take his life just 14 months later. Our four children were already remarkable human beings, aged eight through to 15. Two daughters and two sons.

Sam was 44 years old when he went home to Heaven.

I was suddenly the single mother to four children, and the solo pastor of a Church community. In that place of loss, the Lord gifted each of our children their own revelation of their father's homecoming. He was so good to them. That season was one in which we found the Lord in ways I am convinced we could not have discovered Him otherwise – and perhaps that will be another book for another time.

But I find myself here, today, about to tell you a story of the beauty of family. Writing a book about principles that are unchanging and proven through the fire. Biblical truths that are a firm foundation when everything else is shaken.

I had determined not to remarry. I was content serving the Lord and leading my children. In all honesty, this was the only safe way I could reconcile my future – by eliminating any other potential prospect. But the Lord, in His kindness, had other plans.

Jared was a childhood friend. His parents were the pastors of the Church where my mother and sisters and I first received Christ all those years ago. We grew up in youth ministry together for a few years, before his family moved to another part of the country to follow the call of God, and to pioneer a new Church. We went our separate ways, but stayed loosely connected over the years. In fact, Sam met Jared and his family through the introductions I had made. They communicated occasionally over the twenty years that followed.

When Sam heard that Jared's beautiful wife, Karen, had been diagnosed with a life-threatening disease, he reached out to his friend, offering prayer and support. Soon after, when Jared heard that Sam had been diagnosed with a similar disease, he reciprocated the prayer and support. The two men exchanged messages, phone calls and prayers over the season, when both families were journeying chemotherapy, surgery, and other forms of treatment. Karen eventually went home to be with the Lord, a month before Sam did.

As the seasons progressed, Jared assumed a ministry position in the Church I had continued to lead, and I am sure you can connect the rest of the dots. I will tell the whole story, in all its miracles and all its wonders, some other time in the future. For the sake of this project, I simply want to focus on the conviction and victory that I have received in Jesus. The questioning, aching heart of that 12-year-old girl, from a broken home, has been answered in full by God and His principles, which have proved true regardless of human subtleties, personalities, or earthly circumstances.

Together Jared and I stand in awe of God. I guess one could consider themselves lucky if it only happened once. One strong marriage and family might be a fluke case of chance. However, we have lived – and are living – in the beauty and blessing of family through loss, under two different mantles, in two different seasons, with varying personalities, and adverse circumstances. We are living proof that the Family Altar is God's design. We are living proof that His principles are true. We are living proof that the answer to all the world's problems is found in a healthy God-centred home. When the values of Heaven are central, the fruit is sure.

> *Therefore by their fruits you will know them.*
> *Matthew 7:20 (NKJV)*

So why 'The Family Altar'?

Because I have always believed that family is the first ministry. Today, I am more compelled by this than ever before. Our homes are temples, and our tables are altars. We are kings and priests, and our homes are the foundation of everything we will ever build, or any other arena we may ever assume. The Family Altar is the first place of worship to the Lord, where we lead our spouses and our children into His presence. When that is first, the outflow of our lives will follow their proper ordinances in Him.

> *Do not be deceived, God is not mocked; for whatever a man sows, that he will also reap. For he who sows to his flesh will of the flesh reap corruption, but he who sows to the Spirit will of the Spirit reap everlasting life. And let*

> *us not grow weary while doing good, for in due season we shall reap if we do not lose heart. Therefore, as we have opportunity, let us do good to all, especially to those who are of the household of faith.*
>
> *Galatians 6:7-10 (NKJV)*

When Nehemiah rebuilt the broken walls of the holy city, he commissioned families to do the work. Not army commanders, or construction workers, but families. The work of the rebuild was carried out by families, swiftly and excellently.

Be assured, friend, we are in those days again, when the walls of society have been broken down and they lie in rubble.

A city without walls is susceptible to all kinds of invasion, attack, and plundering. This is our current reality in the world. Marriages and families – and, as a consequence, generations and nations – have been relentlessly ravaged. It is time for families to rebuild. To return home and rebuild.

This is a book of hope. In a generation that has so desperately lost its way, breaking itself against the commandments of God, and abandoning marriage, family, and God's divine plan, this book has a single aim: to restore family to the heart of our culture.

This is my life message. This is my conviction. This is the truth that sets individuals free, and builds nations. I have lived, and continue to live, this truth – a truth that survives tragedy, contradiction, and the onslaught of spiritual opposition.

I am compelled, and have made it my goal over these pages, to restore the foundational Biblical principle of a society founded in marriage and family – so that, in turn, we might rebuild the broken walls of our generation.

SECTION ONE

Valour & Vine

VALOUR & VINE

In the beginning, God established a divine plan for our flourishing. Before time itself, we were on His mind, and in His heart.

Of all the creation He made, man and woman were the only two He reached down, and fashioned with His own hands. In perfect peace, perfect design, and perfect mission, He formed them. They were the masterpiece of all He had made, His greatest delight. The three would find meaning through their connection to each other. The three were perfect in unity – individual and distinguishable, and yet finding perfection in their common union with each other. This was the Creator's intention, and great joy. Perfect man, in his essence, perfect woman in hers, bound together as one in covenantal relationship together with Him.

There are no other genders, and there is no other marriage. This is it. This was and is, and always will be, the created design for human flourishing. This is the place from which life and blessing flow. For reasons we will explore in the pages of this book, we now find ourselves in a conflict, a war against that design.

But conflict was not where it began, and conflict is not our portion. Two gardens – Eden and Gethsemane – hold our answers, and our truth. We must return to those gardens to see the Father's work within them, so that we can live from the plan, and the victory, He set in motion there.

Valour and Vine is the surprising and unexpected journey of the men's and women's ministries within our Church community. Based in the nation of Australia, we sensed a growing dissatisfaction in the Spirit, and knew we needed to enter the fight for manhood and womanhood. We began to recognise the real impact of the feminist movement on both genders, the impact it has had across all of society, and into the coming generations.

In our part of the world, we identified the breakdown of manhood as being the target we wanted to aim for first. And so the Valour ministry was birthed. What a spiritual work it has been.

Two years later, I sensed the invitation to reinstate women's ministry in our Church community as well. I was surprised, as I had initially felt to wait while the men were being profiled and rebuilt. But, when everything began to fall into place for the women's ministry again, I knew the time had come.

The second-century Christian theologian and Church Father, St Irenaeus of Lyons, famously wrote, 'The glory of God is man fully alive'. He beautifully expressed the truth that humanity reaches its fullness, and God is most glorified, when people are in right relationship with Him, and reflect His life and image.

> *The glory of God is man fully alive.*
> *St Irenaeus of Lyons*

> *Then God said, "Let Us make man in Our image, according to Our likeness; let them have dominion over the fish of the sea, over the birds of the air, and over the cattle, over all the Earth and over every creeping thing that creeps on the Earth." So God created man in His own image; in the image of God He created him; male and female He created them.*
> *Genesis 1:26-27 (NKJV)*

Valour and vine. Male and female. His image and His likeness. Where it all began.

VALOUR

Man. The image bearer. Oh, how desperately we need him at his best. Creation aches in the absence of his true presence. He is designed to be the bold, skilful, and responsible steward of humanity. He is our security, our blessing, our strength. He bears the nature of his Creator – good and kind, strong, generous, and faithful. He is a rock, our foundation for flourishing.

Yet he has lost his way. Contemporary culture has led us into a crisis of masculinity, marked by an epidemic of confusion and passivity as the man's identity is lost. The war against him has impacted us all. Men have been emasculated, and the outcome has become either withdrawal and weakness, or domination and self-servitude, both of which are destructive to men, women, and society at large.

Even as I write this, I sense the hiss of the forked tongue. Man, the enemy has lied to you. He has lied about you. Just like womanhood, manhood is not optional; it is design. Without it there is breakdown at large.

Man, you are both king and priest. You are both a disciple of Jesus, and one who makes disciples. You are a warrior, and you are productive. Every time you relinquish who you really are, you are exposing those you were called to love and protect. We need you.

"Come back."

I can hear the Creator's call, "Where are you? Come back."

Come back to design, divine intent, and to flourish.

It is essential to recognise, and teach, that masculinity has a natural design and purpose. Our sons must be given permission to be who they were created to be, not shamed or suppressed for it. True manhood must be formed and discipled in our sons. This is so they can live from it, and be understood and celebrated by our daughters, who will stand alongside them. When masculinity is suppressed, it harms all of society.

This is why it all starts here. When men fail to step into their God-given purpose, families and communities are weakened. Rather than attempting to feminise men, we should be encouraging our boys to harness their natural design so they become the stabilising force our society so desperately needs. We cannot repair marriages, families, or broader social issues, until we rebuild the man.

Adam, we need you to rise.

The term 'man (or men) of valour' appears 37 times in Scripture. The Lord employs this term as a bragging right, and a standard-setter, when recalling these men in His narrative. They were men who did great exploits for the Lord. They understood their mandate, and assumed responsibility on behalf of their families and their communities. They stood tall and did what the occasion demanded of them. They put themselves on the line boldly, sacrificially, resolutely.

> *Be watchful, stand firm in the faith, act like men, be strong.*
>
> *1 Corinthians 16:13 (ESV)*

This has been the foundational Scripture for the men of our Church. As a community we recognise and unapologetically claim that there is a distinct way for men to stand and act across generations. 'Men of valour' is the mandated identity for those male image-bearers in Christ.

> *So when the woman saw that the tree was good for food, that it was pleasant to the eyes, and a tree desirable*

> *to make one wise, she took of its fruit and ate. She also gave to her husband with her, and he ate. Then the eyes of both of them were opened, and they knew that they were naked; and they sewed fig leaves together and made themselves coverings.*
>
> *And they heard the sound of the* Lord *God walking in the garden in the cool of the day, and Adam and his wife hid themselves from the presence of the* Lord *God among the trees of the garden. Then the* Lord *God called to Adam and said to him, "Where are you?"*
>
> *Genesis 3:6-9 (NKJV)*

In Genesis 3, after the fall, God didn't call out to Eve; He called out to Adam. Even though it was Eve who was deceived, God held Adam to account. She was misled and tricked by the serpent, but Adam was called to account. His failure wasn't aggression or oppression, it was passivity. The Creator wanted to know why Adam stood by, in silence, while the serpent deceived his wife. His refusal to act, to lead, to protect, opened the door for sin to enter the human story.

Passivity has been the fatal wound of manhood ever since. In every generation, men are tempted to withdraw, avoid responsibility, and stay silent when clarity and courage are most needed.

And today, when a man does try to lead with that courage and clarity, he's often condemned for it. So, the forked tongue has silenced him, while hissing in the ears of Adam's wife and children. Adam stands silently by, afraid or ashamed of the raw instinct to lead and confront. Yet those are the very qualities God called him to walk in, and expects an account for.

When God came looking for Adam after the fall, He was not merely calling him personally; He was calling him to stand accountable on behalf of both himself and the woman. That moment establishes a foundational truth. Men are held responsible for the leadership and spiritual covering of their families and communities.

God's first question to the fallen man was, "Where are you?" It's still His question to every man today. Where are you in your calling? Where are you in your responsibility? Where are you in your courage?

I once asked Jared what stops him from looking at pornography. Knowing him to be a romantic, I expected him to say something about his love for me, or his commitment to our marriage, but that is not what he said.

"Because I don't want to grieve the Holy Spirit's presence in my life."

I was taken aback and momentarily speechless. This was not what I had expected to hear. It was not even a line of reasoning I had considered in this context. A few hours later, I asked him why he had not mentioned me, or us, in his response.

"Oh, that's a given," he said. "My covenant with you is before the Lord, and so I honour Him in honouring you. I don't want to do anything that breaks my intimacy with Him."

This is the first mandate of manhood – his relationship with the Lord.

In the garden, God visited with man daily. Man was created to walk in communion with the Lord. When man sins, he breaks covenant with God. Sin brings separation and shame, and shame stops us from leading. Shame makes us hide. Hiding removes us from the arena, leaving it void of its main characters. The story fractures, and confusion reigns.

As in the garden, we still retreat – into work, distraction, or isolation. Men pull back from the front line, and from leading with strength. But valour calls men out of hiding, and back into the presence of God – into combat with their enemy, protection of their families, and leadership within their communities.

Adam should have stood up. He should have confronted the serpent, and defended the truth of God's Word, which he had received firsthand. His silence gave deception a voice. In that moment, Adam, the image of spiritual authority and courage, should have crushed the serpent's head. But he did not, and sin entered the story.

But there was a second garden, and a second Adam. Jesus Christ, at the cross, stood in the second garden, and did what the first Adam failed to do. He confronted evil, bore responsibility for another's sin, and crushed the serpent's head once and for all. He broke the curse on man, He broke the curse on woman, and the promise of Genesis 3:15 was fulfilled.

> *He shall bruise your head,*
> *and you shall bruise his heel.*
> *Genesis 3:15 (b) (ESV)*

Jesus modelled active obedience, sacrificial leadership, and valorous love. In Him, men are invited to reclaim the posture of authority, courage, and servant-hearted strength, which was given to them at their origins.

From the very beginning, God gave man a mandate, 'Be fruitful, multiply, fill the Earth, and subdue it' (Genesis 1:28). A man of valour has the fortitude to bring order and flourishing to whatever God entrusts to him. Dominion is not domination. Man is called to subdue, not suppress. It is servant leadership, anchored in the heart of God, which allows men of valour to cultivate life around them, and make things strong – in homes, workplaces, and communities – through righteous leadership and faithful presence.

And remember: Adam was never meant to carry dominion alone. Eve was given as his partner in purpose. Together, they were to reflect the relationship between Christ and the Church, marked by love, respect, and shared mission.

True valour produces fruit, not merely outcomes, and a lasting impact that flows from a man's relationship with God. When a man stays connected to the vine, Christ Himself, his strength, leadership, and fruitfulness will come from intimacy with God, not from his own capacity or vain striving. The manifestation of man's identity flows out of abiding: being in right-relationship with God and with others.

We must expect our boys, and our men, to take risks and to pursue righteousness. At the same time, we must recognise that this is a process, and encourage them to grow into responsibility.

Early in my pregnancy with our third child, before we knew the baby's gender, I had a dream. In it, a man of God visited me in a hospital room as I held my newborn baby. He asked me the child's name.

"Jude," I answered.

"What is his name?" the man of God asked again.

"Jude," I replied a second time.

"What is his name?" he asked once more.

This time I hesitated. I looked at the baby, then back at the man of God.

"Judah," I responded.

At that, the man walked out of the room. I awoke knowing the Lord had named the baby in my womb, and that this child was a son.

Later gender scans revealed the truth of the dream – a boy. A sudden weight of responsibility washed over me. Growing up in a female-dominated household, I was intensely and acutely aware of my inadequacy in raising a man of God.

A second emotion washed over me – a reckoning. I would be his measure for womanhood, and his measure of how a man is to be treated by a woman. My example to him, both as his mother and as a wife, would set the parameters for what he would expect of himself as a man. The responsibility was weighty. I would examine myself, over and over, in the years ahead. I still do.

Who would this child grow to know himself to be? This was now my responsibility as his mother.

We must teach our boys the type of godly character that fosters integrity, resilience, courage, and competence. We must teach them that their natural drives are to be celebrated, and how to discipline those drives, rather than succumb to the pressure to suppress them. We must teach them that their leadership is not oppressive authoritarianism, but servanthood wrapped in courage and wisdom.

To the men and the boys, I want you to hear me: there is nothing toxic about your masculinity. You are not a problem to be solved, or an oppressor to be silenced. You are lovely beyond description. We cherish you. But we need you to stand up. When you do not, we are ravaged and abused.

You have been lied to. We have all been lied to. But the serpent has been crushed, and his forked tongue exposed and silenced. It is time to realign with manhood as your God-design.

We need you.

VINE

What is a woman?

I can hardly believe we have reached this point in history. For all the supposed progress proclaimed over the centuries, it is absolutely beyond my comprehension that we now live in a day where we cannot define what a woman is. Yet the truth is that we can – if we would only go back to Scripture, where our origin and identity are revealed.

In Genesis chapters one, two and three we see woman has been created intentionally and equally valuable to labour with man. Both were made in the image of God. She was designed to be active, powerful, and dynamic, exercising co-authority with man. In the New Testament, we see Jesus' revolutionary treatment of women in the Gospels, as he restores them to the place they held in the garden of Eden.

Jesus' interaction with women was revolutionary because of what was lost in the fall and the subsequent curse passed down. The woman abdicated her authority when she listened to the hiss of the enemy. Man abdicated his. Both came under a curse, especially the woman. And the liar, the deceiver, the serpent, he knows the Scriptures. To this day, as he did at the beginning, he perverts Scripture against humanity. Through deception, he brings people under oppression.

The trouble with being deceived is you don't know you are. This is why it is effective. Only a clear understanding of, and obedience to, God's Word can remedy deception.

The woman became the target of the enemy in the garden – and his ongoing target – because of the curse he received from the Lord. Through God's curse, Satan's demise was prophesied to come through the woman – her Seed would crush his head and he would bruise her Seed's heel.

> *So the LORD God said to the serpent:*
> *"Because you have done this,*
> *You are cursed more than all cattle,*
> *And more than every beast of the field;*
> *On your belly you shall go,*
> *And you shall eat dust*
> *All the days of your life.*
> *And I will put enmity*
> *Between you and the woman,*
> *And between your seed and her Seed;*
> *He shall bruise your head,*
> *And you shall bruise His heel."*
> *Genesis 3:14-15 (NKJV)*

Satan has always hated women. As the master deceiver who perverts the words and plans of God, he has successfully worked to oppress, degrade, and erode womanhood over the generations. The misinterpretation and misapplication of Scripture, together with the deceptive, subtle, and relentless erosion of culture has diminished womanhood in profound ways.. Her lost condition is a result of cultural, societal and spiritual forces at play, all authored by the serpent.

But Jesus found and restored the woman. He restored her in His real-time interactions with women while He walked the earth, and He restored her once and for all in His work on the cross, where every curse was broken.

The cultural and spiritual distortions that women experience come through cultural expectations, media, peer influence, and the misinterpretation of Scripture, all with the intent and effect of diminishing a woman's worth. A woman's strength is diminished, at great cost, while her gentler predispositions towards intuition, nurture and relational nous are treated as weaknesses to be despised rather than embraced as powerful contributions to society.

Relational strength and nurture are core to womanhood, yet the feminist movement has mocked and despised these traits in an effort to make women more masculine. We need women to embrace their womanhood. Even the strongest women with the clearest leadership gifts are also innately nurturers and relational beings.

In all my reading of Scripture, I see women called to leadership and influence, participating actively in the formation and reformation of culture and nations. Generation after generation, I see them changing the world. This theme is prolific in the Scriptures from cover to cover.

To be a woman is not to be less than a man. To be a woman is to be a leader. But to be a woman is also to be tender and discerning. To be a woman in her design is not at the expense of men, the subversion of men, or the dismissal of men. Nor is it to be quiet and hidden, silent and without cultural impact.

Woman's identity and leadership exist in synergy with men, not in competition with them. Wherever that plays out – whether in the home, the workplace, the Church, or society – men and women are called to stand and lead side by side as equal, co-reigning heirs on mission together.

I have often heard it said that the woman is the heart of the home, and this truth came alive in my spirit when I saw it in Scripture.

> *Your wife shall be like a fruitful vine*
> *In the very heart of your house,*
> *Your children like olive plants*
> *All around your table.*
> *Psalm 128:3 (NKJV)*

There is such beauty for her to behold and become. I believe this passage extends beyond the conventional idea of home into the wider spaces where men and women interact – workplaces, Churches, and cultural environments. Woman is often the heart of her environment, bringing beauty to those around her. In her healthiest state, she is fruitful and holds the hearts of everyone in her proximity.

I revel in the imagery of a vine that grows and stretches and reaches out in every direction. It buds and brings life wherever it goes. I love the context of the vine within the covering of a home, filling that space with vitality, vibrance, and flourishing. Together with man, woman creates environments of flourishing. He provides the context; she provides the heart. He provides the structure, while she brings life to the soul within.

Ultimately, that union between man and woman is connected to the true Vine, Jesus, like the binding together of the three-strand cord (Ecclesiastes 4:12) – inseparable and life-giving to one other. He is the ultimate source of our flourishing as we connect to Him and come from Him.

> *I am the Vine, you are the branches. He who abides in Me, and I in him, bears much fruit; for without Me you can do nothing.*
> *John 15:5 (NKJV)*

Together, the three form a powerful bond, initiated and intended by the very heart of the Everlasting Father from the beginning of time. There is an order He has prescribed for the flourishing of each environment and, consequently, for the collective generations shaped within them.

Walk With Us

What is at stake here is intergenerational. Identity is transmitted from one generation to the next, so it is imperative that we can clearly define man and woman. Mothers and grandmothers, fathers and grandfathers, even mentors, must rise as strong role models for that effective transmission to take place from one generation to the next.

The hour is late. It is time for men and women to actively take up the mandate of setting a godly example for the rising generation – because the war against their identity has reached unprecedented intensity. There is no more time for mothers and fathers, grandmothers and grandfathers, for the big brothers and sisters, or the midwives of faith, to sit back and allow culture to do the work they were responsible to do on behalf of the next generation.

It is time for Titus 2 men and women to rise in strength, with the mission burdening their hearts towards action as their supreme priority, without reserve.

> *But as for you, speak the things which are proper for sound doctrine: that the older men be sober, reverent, temperate, sound in faith, in love, in patience; the older women likewise, that they be reverent in behaviour, not slanderers, not given to much wine, teachers of good things – that they admonish the young women to love their husbands, to love their children, to be discreet, chaste, homemakers, good, obedient to their own husbands, that the word of God may not be blasphemed.*
>
> *Likewise, exhort the young men to be sober-minded, in all things showing yourself to be a pattern of good works; in doctrine showing integrity, reverence, incorruptibility, sound speech that cannot be condemned, that one who is an opponent may be ashamed, having nothing evil to say of you.*
>
> *Titus 2:1-8 (NKJV)*

Something strange has happened to the older generation in recent years. The Covid pandemic taught us to withdraw and isolate ourselves from others. We were convinced that turning inward was the necessary means to survival. Not only is this the opposite message of the Gospel of self-denial but, as a result, a wide yawning gorge has formed between the generations. Mothers, fathers, grandmothers, and grandfathers, have disappeared from the leadership landscape of culture. They are fearful. They are numbing themselves. They are planning retirement, and caravan escapes along coastlines. They have disconnected from their mandate to love and lead the next generation.

I often ask them for help. I invite them to press into community, and draw the younger generations closer, only to be met with preoccupation, preference management or reluctance. They are busy in the insulated lives they are building. We desperately lack their example and connection. We are missing their wisdom and sacrifice. The cavernous gorge is deep and dangerous.

To the older women: I implore you to open your home and your life. Get alone in the presence of God and ask Him to awaken you again – He will burden you with an urgency for the next generation. Bring in the younger women, because they are desperately asking questions that no generation in the past has had to ask, or find answers to. You are their only hope. Please make this a priority. Please hear my invitation to take seriously the Titus 2 call on this season of your life.

To the older men: godly adult male role models must come to the fore. We need to see you, and hear you. We need you to lead the next generation of men out of passivity, into lives that are fully engaged with their God-given purpose. In a culture that suppresses masculine leadership, that feminises boys, that overprotects them, and asserts that the natural drive and aggression in the heart of a boy is pathologically wrong, we need Godly men to disciple the instincts in younger men, to realign with their God-given design.

To the younger men and women: be careful where you are sourcing your advice. If the books and podcasts you are consuming around marriage, parenting, and identity, are produced by people who are not Spirit-filled, born-again believers, then you need to switch them off, and turn them aside.

> *But the natural man does not receive the things of the Spirit of God, for they are foolishness to him; nor can he know them, because they are spiritually discerned.*
> *1 Corinthians 2:14 (NKJV)*

> *For the wisdom of this world is foolishness with God. For it is written, "He catches the wise in their own craftiness";*
> *1 Corinthians 3:19 (NKJV)*

Being a man or a woman of God, being a mother or father, a wife or husband, are the most spiritual things you will ever do. Don't look to the psychology of the world – it is rigged against you and the seed coming through you. Worldly wisdom does not recognise, or understand, the things of the Spirit. In fact, the spirit of the age is relentlessly warring against the Kingdom of Heaven. All the wisdom of the world will end up being sheer foolishness, and extremely costly, if it takes the seat of authority in the life of a Jesus-follower. Instead, a believer should proactively, and relentlessly, seek out Godly wisdom in Scripture, and in the counsel of proven godly women, men, pastors, leaders, and authors, for your guidance, who have lived lives in the Spirit built on Scripture.

The restoration of manhood and womanhood will only be achieved by embracing the truth of Scripture. That alignment with God's design is the only path back. To fulfil our design as women alongside men, we need to reclaim our God-given male or female identity, and step boldly into the places of leadership and influence that were ordained for us in that first garden (in our design before the curse) and reinstated to us in the second garden (when the curse was broken).

The Full Image Of God

Now more than ever, I am convinced that the Lord esteems the marriage union as the highest of all relationships on this side of eternity.

Marriage – a bride and her bridegroom – are the images the Lord chooses to use when He illustrates His commitment to humanity throughout the generations of all history past, present, and yet to come. He describes the Church as His Bride. He describes us as His Beloved. He describes Himself as the Bridegroom.

The Lord is jealous over the institution of marriage, which is why it is under relentless, unending attack. He gave marriage to humanity as a gift for best flourishing, and to exercise blessed dominion in the generations. Marriage is precious to the Lord.

Marriage is sacred. It is the giving and receiving of two individuals to each other in covenant under God. It is holy and it carries the seeds of Heaven. I am convinced that the answer to all the world's problems is found in a healthy marriage, and a healthy home. The fallout we see in society comes back to the breakdown of these bonds.

When I sit with politicians to ask where the lion's share of their time is devoted, they usually point to social issues – homelessness, substance abuse, crime, and violence. They spend their days developing and deploying policies to address these problems. When I press the issue further, and ask what lies at the root of it all, they are unanimous – it starts early, and it starts at home.

Of all the Band-Aid solutions that politicians can offer their constituents, the true answer is found in the home – the heart of God for humanity; His two image-bearers in union and oneness, exercising their God-given authority.

> *Then God said, "Let Us make man in Our image, according to Our likeness; let them have dominion over the fish of the sea, over the birds of the air, and over the cattle, over all the Earth and over every creeping thing that creeps on the Earth."* ***So God created man in His***

own image; in the image of God He created him; male and female He created them. *Then God blessed them, and God said to them, "Be fruitful and multiply; fill the Earth and subdue it; have dominion over the fish of the sea, over the birds of the air, and over every living thing that moves on the earth."*

And God said, "See, I have given you every herb that yields seed which is on the face of all the Earth, and every tree whose fruit yields seed; to you it shall be for food. Also, to every beast of the earth, to every bird of the air, and to everything that creeps on the earth, in which there is life, I have given every green herb for food"; and it was so. Then God saw everything that He had made, and indeed it was very good. So the evening and the morning were the sixth day.

Genesis 1:26-31 (NKJV)

And the LORD God caused a deep sleep to fall on Adam, and he slept; and He took one of his ribs, and closed up the flesh in its place. Then the rib which the LORD God had taken from man He made into a woman, and He brought her to the man.

And Adam said:
"This is now bone of my bones
And flesh of my flesh;
She shall be called Woman,
Because she was taken out of Man."

Therefore a man shall leave his father and mother and be joined to his wife, and they shall become ***one flesh****. And they were both naked, the man and his wife, and were not ashamed.*

Genesis 2:21-25 (NKJV)

So much meaning is encapsulated in these verses. Man and woman are uniquely and perfectly fashioned in the image, and likeness, of their Creator – male and female, created to reflect His nature. We are blessed and mandated for multiplication. We are given dominion and delegated authority over our surroundings, and we carry this inheritance and authority as co-equal stewards.

While we are both image bearers, our two created forms, male and female, are distinctly different from each other. While we are both uniquely complete, it is in our union together that the full glory of God is revealed. We are not designed, or called, to compete with each other. We are co-equal, co-labourers, co-heirs, and co-executors of the Will of God in the Earth. Each carries authority. Each carries dominion. Together we carry the image and likeness of God. Each carries the seed of the other.

When these two dynamic creatures come together in covenant, their united oneness carries supernatural power. It is in this unified oneness that the image-bearers have the power to multiply. While distinct and whole in themselves, they cannot multiply without each other. This is fascinating. Their divine mandate to multiply is fulfilled only by their coming together. This is supernatural. There is nothing like it in the Earth.

And so the enemy rages against it. Not only does he wage war against their union; he wages war against their unique image. So we see the attack on gender and function.

The sacredness of design has been the subject of a degeneration like no other, to the point where leaders and politicians today can no longer define a man or a woman. Our personhood has been stolen from us and marred by lies. Confusion reigns, and the breakdown has fractured further and further into the heart of each subsequent generation.

In turn, the two have been taught to mistrust each other. Doubtful about their own value and sacredness, they are also sceptical of the other. Having lost themselves, man and woman are now turning on each other. How I ache with grief as I witness couple after couple, where one or both spouses are desperately protecting self-interests, hurling accusations and attacks at the very one they are tethered to in the Spirit. Oblivious to recognise they are damaging themselves, as they damage the other. I grieve watching spouses pursue self-oriented exploits at the expense of the multiplied synergy they could be experiencing in oneness with their beloved.

> Now *the serpent was more cunning than any beast of the field which the* LORD *God had made. And he said to the woman, "Has God indeed said, 'You shall not eat of every tree of the garden'?"*
>
> *And the woman said to the serpent, "We may eat the fruit of the trees of the garden; but of the fruit of the tree which is in the midst of the garden, God has said, 'You shall not eat it, nor shall you touch it, lest you die.'"*
>
> *Then the serpent said to the woman, "You will not surely die. For God knows that in the day you eat of it your eyes will be opened, and you will be like God, knowing good and evil."*
>
> *So when the woman saw that the tree was good for food, that it was pleasant to the eyes, and a tree desirable to make one wise, she took of its fruit and ate. She also gave to her husband with her, and he ate.*
>
> *Genesis 3:1-6 (NKJV)*

It was always the enemy's plan to come between the woman and the man. He addressed Eve, deceived her, and she usurped Adam's authority. The serpent may not have directly spoken to Adam, but his goal was to weaken him through the woman. By appealing to her softer nature, he came between them, and brought them both down together.

There must be oneness and unity within a marriage covenant. Unless man and woman are together in mutual submission, and humility, before each other under God's Word, their union will come under all types of strife and breakdown. Husband and wife are called to each other for life, to the exclusion of all others, and bound together in the Lord. A three-strand cord that is strong to withstand breaking.

> *But from the beginning of the creation, God 'made them male and female.' 'For this reason a man shall leave his father and mother and be joined to his wife, and the two shall become one flesh'; so then they are no longer two, but one flesh.* ***Therefore what God has joined together, let not man separate.***
> *Mark 10:6-9 (NKJV)*

They must fight for unity. They must remember that they belong to each other, not to themselves. They must come back to a place of deference and submission to one another. To love the other is to love oneself. To hurt the other is to hurt oneself. They are to become one to the point where they are individual and yet indivisible. They are one.

> *Though one may be overpowered by another, two can withstand him.*
> *And a threefold cord is not quickly broken.*
> *Ecclesiastes 4:12 (NKJV)*

They are called to be bound together under an equal yoke, where they are side-by-side, functioning in the Earth as the Lord's executors with His delegated authority. They are fruitful out of their oneness.

Man and woman were given their ordinance at the time of creation (Genesis 1:26-31). They were called to be industrious, faithful stewards of the creation which God had made and given to them for care. They were given charge of the dominion. They were given delegated authority. They were co-equals, and they were co-heirs. They were called to live into the mandate together.

Friend, allow yourself to be lost in the wonder of it. He is the image of the Lord. She is the image of the Lord. Together there is an explosion of dynamic supernatural mandate ushered into the natural realm. How blessed we are, how entrusted we are, how infinitely close we are to our Creator when we step into the fullness of this blessing and mandate.

Chosen

When your personal experience of reality in the family home is divorce (as is the case for the majority today), there is always a shadow of a sneaking premonition that it may be your fate also. Statistics prove it is likely to become reality. The fear of potential rejection, and abandonment, by a spouse one day is never far. It was one of the first questions I asked when I accepted Sam's proposal at the age of 19.

"Will you ever fall out of love with me?"

His response was so adamant and immediate that it shocked me.

"No."

"How can you be so sure?" I asked in response.

"Because love is not a feeling, love is a choice," he replied.

In my typical strong-headed way, I pushed back, "So you're saying you're going to have to *choose* to love me?"

He smiled and said, "Judging by that response, no doubt some days I will."

And that was that. In the years that followed I learned that marriage truly is a choice, and a covenant, that is not to be broken. My husband modelled in his commitment to me the same choice Christ makes with us.

> ***You didn't choose me. I chose you.***
> *John 15:16 (NLT)*
>
> *Just as He* ***chose us in Him before the foundation of the world****, that we should be holy and without blame before Him in love*
> *Ephesians 1:4 (NKJV)*

> *But God demonstrates His own love toward us,* ***in that while we were still sinners, Christ died for us.***
> *Romans 5:8 (NKJV)*

I learned what it truly meant to be chosen on the merits of the one making the choice, not on the merits of my own condition. His commitment would be unwavering. This is the mandate for a husband to live by.

I was chosen, and would be chosen every day, by both my Saviour and my husband. Even when I was difficult to love, even when I fell short, even when I didn't feel worthy. My husband was an extension, and the example, of Christ's love towards me. When I eventually learned to live in the fullness of this reality, I found myself with the capacity to be able to extend that same grace and love to others.

There is something important to be said about the initial choosing process. Scripture is also beautifully clear on how to make the initial choice.

> *Do not be unequally yoked together with unbelievers. For what fellowship has righteousness with lawlessness? And what communion has light with darkness? And what accord has Christ with Belial (the devil)? Or what part has a believer with an unbeliever? And what agreement has the temple of God with idols? For you are the temple of the living God.*
> *2 Corinthians 6:14-16 (NKJV)*

If I could sit with every young person before they make a choice for a life partner, I could not stress this Scripture enough. I would tell them of the countless people I've walked with, who would plead that they chose well. I could tell you about both men and women, who bound themselves with another person in an unequal yoke. I could tell you of their pain. I could tell you of the pain and the fallout in their children. I would even suggest to you that it would be better for you to stay single, than connect yourself to the wrong person.

However, I have seen the opposite to be true also. I have seen two very unremarkable people join together, heading in the same direction with a wholehearted pursuit after God, become the most remarkable of spiritual forces.

To my daughter, I would say, wait! Wait for the man who knows who he is in the Lord. Wait for a man of virtue who has consecrated himself to the Lord. Who understands, with a deep conviction, the power of his purity and his honour. Darling, he does exist. He is remarkable, pure and inspiring. Wait for him.

Wait for the man who will esteem you, and preserve you in your beauty and dignity. Wait for the man who can deny himself for the sake of your virtue. Wait for the man who is burning with a passion for God. If he is not going to lead you and your future children in the Lord, don't even give him another thought. Wait, darling.

Wait for the man who has work ethic and vision. A man of high repute, who speaks with the tongues of angels. I would echo the words of the late Charlie Kirk who said, "Men, expect more from yourselves. Women, expect more from your men."

To my son I would say, be on guard against the lures of the girl who is vying for attention. Who dresses and behaves in a way that aims to turn heads, and reveals more than what is tasteful.

> *Don't talk to me of female beauty, rather virtues of her soul. A beautiful woman, who has not decorated herself with virtue, is like a painted coffin.*
> *St John Chrysostom*

Darling son, avoid drama and the one who tries to lock you up in deep conversation, luring you to herself and away from your meaningful contribution to the world. Instead look for the one who is busy in her own calling. Whose beauty radiates from within. Who stimulates your mind, not just your senses. Who is quieter than the raging, raucous obscenity around her. Who is serving Jesus, not simply appearances. Who is humble and gentle. Who is generous. Who is wise.

I would suggest that she would be the type of girl whose heart is reserved deep within the Lord Himself. As Maya Angelou said, her heart would be so hidden in the Lord that you have to seek the Lord just to find her. That is the one to choose.

> *A woman's heart should be so hidden in God that a man has to seek Him just to find her.*
> *Maya Angelou*

My sons and my daughters, when you find that person, make the Lord the centre of your orbit together, and the sole focus of your vision. The more engaged you become with each other, the more engaged you should be in the things and the purposes of Heaven. Don't ever pull back to build your own kingdom; only and always build the Kingdom of Heaven together. Choose well – because your whole future is at stake.

Of course, there is always a grace for those who find the Lord later in life. He is all-encompassing, ever powerful, and all sufficient. Of course He sees you if you find Him after you have lived a life away from the Lord, and outside of His plans. And to the person who has an unbelieving spouse, the Lord has a plan. You can trust Him.

> *Now, I will speak to the rest of you, though I do not have a direct command from the Lord. If a fellow believer has a wife who is not a believer and she is willing to continue living with him, he must not leave her. And if a believing woman has a husband who is not a believer and he is willing to continue living with her, she must not leave him. For the believing wife brings holiness to her marriage, and the believing husband brings holiness to his marriage. Otherwise, your children would*

> *not be holy, but now they are holy. (But if the husband or wife who isn't a believer insists on leaving, let them go. In such cases the believing husband or wife is no longer bound to the other, for God has called you to live in peace.) Don't you wives realise that your husbands might be saved because of you? And don't you husbands realise that your wives might be saved because of you?*
>
> *1 Corinthians 7:12-16 (NLT)*

Covered

My home, in the teenage years, was a female-only domain – a single mum, two younger sisters, and even the pet dog was female. That early environment shaped the views I had on the roles of men and women, and influenced my personal life experiences and expectations.

As a young wife, twenty years of age, longing for a healthy marriage under the pattern of Heaven, I realised very quickly that I needed to shift my thinking. God's Word retrained my understanding of covering, covenant, authority, and submission. At that tender age, I learned Biblical principles that I found were not heavy or oppressive as the world had suggested, but powerful and life-giving. I learned quickly that God's intention for submission was for the good of my family, my children, and my destiny.

The cultural tension we face today is a result of feminism. Initially it may have aimed to address inequality and oppression, but today it often leads to the rejection of men, or seeks to exert control over men. Women are asking why the men won't lead – while they silence and reject the men in their lives.

Feminism has emasculated men. It has silenced and replaced men. It has eroded society by undermining family and gender. Feminism has achieved what it celebrates as the sexual liberation of women. The fruit of these choices has created homes where children are born outside of wedlock, without committed parents present. Both sons and daughters are being raised by single parents, where God's design of leadership by co-equal co-heirs in mutual submission to one another is missing completely.

Often if the men are still at the table, they sit silently, afraid to speak or lead. Children are confused, and unrestrained. Marriages and families are detrimentally weakened. We have sons who don't know how to be men. We have daughters who are growing up without value. Both become adults who don't know how to lead their own lives, or how to lead their children. And the cycle of pain and dysfunction perpetuates. A deep rent runs right through the heart of the fabric of society, deepening with each generation.

I am a strong woman, with a leadership gift, and I have found that God's principles of submission and order do not diminish who I am. In fact, the beauty of God's order for marriage is the very launchpad for my flourishing. The Lord was not surprised as my strength and leadership gifts have emerged over the years. He didn't accidentally question the way He formed me in the depths of the secret place of the womb. He did not wonder if He had put the wrong gifts inside my female frame.

Ultimately, we are not talking about gifts or personalities, we are talking about Spiritual dynamics. A dynamic union where both male and female exhibit their strongest traits, as co-equals in the Kingdom of God, in mutual submission and preference to one another. They are the reflection of the image of God when they become one.

Spiritual covering was important for me to learn, because I was obnoxious and rebellious. I was independent. As my mind was renewed in the Scriptures, I realised that the source of these motivations came from a place of fear, rather than strength. Rebellion and independence were a subconscious and successful means of self-protection that stemmed from my pain. It was also a way of me helplessly asserting myself in an environment that felt like it was a man's world. I sensed there were things in me that could serve others, but I often moved ahead on my own, trying to put forward what I thought was valuable.

It played out in a million little ways. When we were renovating our first home, I would insist on my preference in the way that things should be done. The way the tiles would be laid. The order of the trades that would come in to do the work. The interviewing process as we saw quotes from different carpenters. I controlled everything. Then, one day, I distinctly remember the Holy Spirit saying to me, "What difference does it make which way it is done, if you achieve the common goal?"

I was stopped in my tracks. I immediately felt my heart change, and the weight of pressure I had carried by controlling outcomes suddenly lifted from my shoulders. I loved my husband, and I trusted his unique genius. Why would I control him? From that day, I no longer needed to be the one with all the answers, and all the advice. It was easy, and a joy to follow his lead. I was so blessed to watch us achieve far greater things than I could have done with the suppressive approach I had previously employed.

As an additional and subsequent result, honour has become one of my values. I learned it after years of pain. I learned it after watching dysfunction, where dishonour, self-service, self-protection, and opinion projection, were the norm. I learned by trusting God at His Word. I learned that honour is the pathway to order and blessing. Honour brings order. Honour brings the possibility of miracles closer. Honour releases people to be at their very best, and is a two-way street.

> ***Honour all people***. *Love the brotherhood. Fear God. Honour the king.*
>
> *1 Peter 2:17 (NKJV)*

We are all called to honour others. We are called to mutual submission, mutual deference, and preference to one another. There is a grace for this type of living that is supremely beyond any human striving effort; it is a supernatural principle that always bears good fruit. The self-serving tendencies of the flesh are limited and painful, damaging self and others but, with the grace of the Holy Spirit and the prompting of the living Scriptures, we can live in an entirely different way.

Wives, we are covered by our husbands. There is a supernatural blessing in that covering. I have learned to submit to the covering, and learn to live in the covering.

> *Wives, submit to your own husbands, as to the Lord. For the husband is head of the wife, as also Christ is head of the Church; and He is the Saviour of the body. Therefore, just as the Church is subject to Christ, so let the wives be to their own husbands in everything. Husbands, love your wives, just as Christ also loved the Church and gave Himself for her.*
>
> *Ephesians 5:22-25 (NKJV)*

I have seen many women offended with this passage of Scripture. If they would only allow themselves to be more vulnerable to the truth in it, they would have embraced it wholeheartedly, with deep joy and an expectation of blessing. But the feminist culture has crept into the Church, as well as the world, and finds this offensive because the beauty of it has been perverted. They simply do not understand.

I have seen families come into our Churches and receive Christ with such joy and excitement, crying tears of revelation in the Church gatherings. Then, suddenly and abruptly, they become assaulted in the stronghold of their minds when they begin catching sight of these truths.

I have seen women pull their whole families out of Church over this. The common theme of their reasoning is usually something along the lines that says they have sadly realised their values do not align with the Biblical ones. How my heart aches. I want to cry out, "YES! That's absolutely right! That's the whole point!"

Ultimately, it's the parable of the sower, and the seed and the four types of soil at play here. Sow good seed into a soil that is either distracted, or filled with choking weeds, and the good fruit is terminated before it comes into fruition. The whole point of our discipleship journey in Jesus is that, when we find those exact places of misalignment in our hearts, we learn to realign our hearts in submission to the Word of God. His principles are not suppressive, but for our best flourishing. It was Elizabeth Elliott who said:

> *We must quit bending the Word to suit our situation.*
> *It is we who must be bend to that Word.*
> *Elizabeth Elliot*

And this is for our best flourishing. The Lord is the all-knowing, eternal Master Designer, Who created us out of dust as the beloved of His heart, and the apple of His eye. His mandates for our life are always in our best interests. When we live in accordance with the Scriptures, we live the lives we were made to live; we flourish and we thrive.

There is a special anointing on manhood for the role of covering. Man is not superior. He is not more favoured in the eyes of the Lord. He simply holds the office of covering in the marriage, and in the home. That is his God-ordained role. One day he will stand before the Lord, and give an account for the way that he held that office. The wife will not be accountable for that role. The husband will be. Did he cover and protect her? Did he cover and protect his children? Was he the priest of the home? Was he Christ to his family? It is a weighty responsibility, and one that she will never be accountable for – only he will be.

It is a Spiritual and a Biblical principle. Of course the gift of freewill means that every single one of us has the prerogative to decide whether we will live by it or not. As with all the Spiritual laws, our opinion does not impact on its truth. Just as the atheist who insists that God does not exist, does not make God cease to exist. Like a person trying to argue that gravity is not an infallible natural law, we find ourselves in a place where our believing does not impact the truth of Spiritual laws, nor will the principles and blessings that flow through them fail to bear fruit when applied.

Each person is entitled to believe and live what they choose. They will also live in the harvest of their choices. There is a reason that this Spiritual principle works so beautifully in our natural experience, found in the subsequent verses of that same passage.

> *Husbands, love your wives, just as Christ also loved the Church and gave Himself for her, that He might sanctify and cleanse her with the washing of water by the Word, that He might present her to Himself a glorious Church, not having spot or wrinkle or any such thing, but that she should be holy and without blemish. So husbands ought to love their own wives as their own bodies; he who loves his wife loves himself.*
> *Ephesians 5:25-28 (NKJV)*

The brilliant author CS Lewis depicted it more perfectly than any other way I've seen. He writes:

> *The husband is the head of the wife just in so far as he is to her what Christ is to the Church. He is to love her as Christ loved the Church. This headship, then, is most fully embodied not in the husband we should all wish to be but in him whose marriage is most like a crucifixion; whose wife receives most and gives least, is most unworthy of him, is – in her own mere nature – least loveable. For the Church has no beauty but what the Bridegroom gives her, he does not find, but makes her lovely… As Christ sees in the flawed, proud, fanatical or lukewarm Church on earth that Bride who will one day be without spot or wrinkle, and labours to produce the latter, so the husband whose headship is Christlike (and he is allowed no other sort) never despairs. He is a King Cophetua who*

> *after twenty years still hopes that the beggar-girl will one day learn to speak the truth and wash behind her ears.*
> *C.S Lewis, The Four Loves*

The headship of a man, in the marriage union, is in its full effect when it is the most like a crucifixion. Yes, wives are to submit to their husbands, but husbands are called to die. In his dying, she becomes more beautiful than she could ever have been by her own efforts, or by asserting and protecting herself.

Friends, we must be discerning. The enemy always twists and perverts the things of God. He is the master pervert on a mission to steal, kill, and destroy.

> *The thief does not come except to steal, and to kill, and to destroy. I have come that they may have life, and that they may have it more abundantly.*
> *John 10:10 (NKJV)*

The thief has taken the concept of submission and headship, and twisted it into such a thing that it becomes an offence, and stumbling block, to God's sons and daughters. Do not fall into this trap set by the enemy of your soul.

My late husband, Sam, celebrated me for almost twenty years, and my husband, Jared, is doing the same today. I have been drawn out of myself. I've been promoted, and pushed into the light. I have become who I am through his leadership, and I do my best to draw the potential out of him too. We have both mutually submitted, and mutually died, for the promotion of the other person. It is the mutually submissive, self-sacrificial Jesus in us, and before us, that makes us beautiful. It is the gift of another person's selflessness that brings out the best in us. Marriage is the best earthly example the Lord could use to describe the love Christ has for His Church, His Bride. Marriage is more important to God than any other union on the Earth.

It takes great bravery to accept gifts like this. For the husband to accept the gift of headship. For the wife to accept the gift of submission. Christ offers them both to us daily. He models for us a life that says, "I have died for you, that you might fully live. I was disfigured so that you would become beautiful."

Cleaving

> *But from the beginning of the creation, God 'made them male and female.' 'For this reason a man shall leave his father and mother and be joined to his wife, and the two shall become one flesh'; so then they are no longer two, but one flesh.* ***Therefore what God has joined together, let not man separate.***
>
> *Mark 10:6-9 (NKJV)*

Perhaps the most pointed of all the lessons, Jared and I have learned, has been that of leaving and cleaving. Not once, but twice.

We were both so young when we married our first spouses. I remember how excited I was to start a new family line with Sam. I was excited to cleave to my husband, and to learn together with him the new ways that we would form and build for our family. Cleaving was an exciting fresh start; and that cleaving was effective and strong. We became one in every sense. The fruit of our oneness was evident in all the things we did.

When he went home to be with a Lord, I felt that deep loneliness, and separation, that I had feared as a young girl. I had woken up in the reality I had feared from my childhood, not by rejection but by death. As a daughter of God, I was living in the reality I thought I would be immune from. All my beliefs were thrown into question.

I learned that some questions do not have answers on this side of eternity. I learned not to ask 'why' but to ask 'what now'. On one beautiful morning in the Word, only a few short weeks after Sam had passed, God's promise came flooding into my heart.

> *Do not fear, for you will not be ashamed;*
> *Neither be disgraced, for you will not be put to shame;*
> *For you will forget the shame of your youth,*
> *And will not remember the reproach of your widowhood anymore.*
>
> ***For your Maker is your husband,***
> *The LORD of hosts is His name;*
> *And your Redeemer is the Holy One of Israel;*
> *He is called the God of the whole Earth.*
>
> *For the LORD has called you*
> *Like a woman forsaken and grieved in spirit,*
> *Like a youthful wife when you were refused,"*
> *Says your God.*
>
> *"For a mere moment I have forsaken you,*
> *But with great mercies I will gather you.*
>
> *With a little wrath I hid My face from you for a moment;*
> *But with everlasting kindness I will have mercy on you,"*
> *Says the LORD, your Redeemer.*
> *Isaiah 54:4-8 (NKJV)*

Suddenly, the comfort of the Holy Spirit ministered to me. I realised widowhood was, in itself, a gift, seeing as I now knew I would always have the greatest of husbands in the Lord. Here He was promising Himself to me, in the stillness of a quiet holiday cottage while the children slept, with the Scriptures open on my lap. He took me as His own. I felt the rush of love and peace. I felt His intimate nearness, and His all-encompassing cover. I was home again, in Him.

Of course, I did not realise at the time that His intention for me also included the earlier verses in the first part of that chapter.

> *"Sing, O barren,*
> *You who have not borne!*
> *Break forth into singing, and cry aloud,*
> *You who have not laboured with child!*
> ***For more are the children of the desolate***
> ***Than the children of the married woman,"*** *says the LORD.*
>
> *"Enlarge the place of your tent,*
> *And let them stretch out the curtains of your dwellings;*
> *Do not spare;*
> *Lengthen your cords,*
> *And strengthen your stakes.*
>
> *For you shall expand to the right and to the left,*
> ***And your descendants will inherit the nations,***
> ***And make the desolate cities inhabited.***
> *Isaiah 54: 1-4 (NKJV)*

My singing would not only replace a spirit of heaviness with a garment of praise, but it would also extend the capacity of my heart beyond anything I could ever have prepared for or imagined. How could I ever have known, as that barren-hearted 12-year-old girl, that one day my heart would be the welcome home to seven aching children, and an international community of spiritual sons and daughters.

Jared and I found ourselves at the altar of covenant again. This time, the season was remarkably different. We were not two young people with nothing to lose. We were grown adults, with dependants, reputations, ministries, and experiences. Everything was at stake. We knew the breath of God that day at the altar, standing under nine palm trees by the water, with our friends witnessing His kindness in motion. And we would start again.

We would learn what leaving and cleaving would mean the second time around. This time we were not only leaving our family of origin, we would also now leave the God-ordained beauty we had separately built over two decades, in order to build the new thing the Lord was placing before us. Can I tell you, leaving and cleaving was never so real as it was the second time around? And can I tell you, the Lord's holy Scriptures remain true still?

Do not remember the former things,
Nor consider the things of old.

Behold, I will do a new thing,
Now it shall spring forth;
Shall you not know it?
I will even make a road in the wilderness
And rivers in the desert.

The beast of the field will honour Me,
The jackals and the ostriches,
Because I give waters in the wilderness
And rivers in the desert,
To give drink to My people, My chosen.

This people I have formed for Myself;
They shall declare My praise.
Isaiah 43:18-21 (NKJV)

I have learned this truth: we do not move on, but we must move forward. There are some things we can never move on from – people who are irreplaceable, legacies to be preserved, imprints on our lives that make us who we will always be – but it is a moving forward we must do. Our God is a God of forward motion. In Him, the latter days are always greater than the former. Through trial and test, He is the redeemer, restorer, and Victorious One.

Any person who goes into marriage recognises that they are walking into a covenant that will inevitably be wrought with difficulty. Both parties are imperfect people. The potential for pain and conflict is assured. We proceed by voluntarily choosing to restrain ourselves, in order to become one. We choose to accept a selfless approach towards the other person.

> *Imperfect people, helping imperfect people, is God's perfect plan.*
> *Tommy Barnett*

The active choice of binding ourselves together, regardless of what may come or what lay behind, is the key to deepening the love between those two parties. If the back door is open, if commitment is optional, casual, or indolent, then the love will be shallow. Only a brave person dares venture into it. It is holy before the Lord. We commit to each other. We agree to stay together, even in the times when we want to flee. Marriage is the greenhouse where our true selves can be grown, often through discomfort.

The Weight Of Honour

How is it that we continue honouring our past, and our families of origin, when we join and cleave to our spouse? All of us have, at least, seen if not experienced the conflict that can happen when the leaving is not successfully achieved in a mutually respectful and honouring way. Sometimes people cling tightly to the things of the past. Other times we see in-laws having a hard time releasing their loved children into their new family. There are various reasons for this, which the Spirit can reveal through prayer and Scripture.

In his incredible book, *Hillbilly Elegy*, JD Vance explores the idea that people from broken backgrounds find this especially difficult. He brilliantly describes the cycles of dysfunction that continue with families, where false loyalty emerges in an attempt to justify, and even celebrate, dysfunction as virtue. In these families, the word honour is used as a form of manipulation or control, whenever a person tries to break free from the things that are broken within their structure. Thankfully, not everyone fights this battle but, for the ones who do, it is sheer agony. The key is in understanding the proper definitions of honour in Scripture, both the Hebrew and the Greek.

In light of the fifth commandment of God, this is breakthrough for the next generation, for both those who come from godly backgrounds, as well as those who come from broken and dysfunctional ones.

> *Honour your father and your mother, that your days may be long upon the land which the* L*ORD your God is giving you.*
> *Exodus 20:12 (NKJV)*

The primary Hebrew word, translated as honour in the Old Testament, is *kavod*. Literally translated, it means to 'give weight to', or 'to measure the heaviness of a thing'.

The Greek word for honour is *timao*. The literal translation is 'to value, esteem or give weight to something'. Again, the same meaning. To honour is to give due weight, due value, and due esteem, to a thing or person.

This is the path to light, life and increase. To truly honour something is to recognise its weight. When we measure its weight, we measure its impact. In the sense of relationships, true honour is to recognise the impact, and the way it bears on the parties within that relationship union. For healthy forward motion, I acknowledge the weight that my past has played in my life – both the good and the bad. It is only when I can truly honour the good, and bad, in a relationship that I can move forward in healthy ways.

But from the beginning of the creation, God 'made them male and female.' 'For this reason a man shall leave his father and mother and be joined to his wife, and the two shall become one flesh'; so then they are no longer two, but one flesh. ***Therefore what God has joined together, let not man separate.***

Mark 10:6-9 (NKJV)

These are the words of Jesus, who drew back on the account in Genesis. These are His words – our saviour, our friend. We leave our father and our mother to become one flesh with our spouse. Jesus added one thing: let no man separate what God joins together. In the new marriage union, a new family has been forged, and made one, in the Lord under holy covenant. The primary spiritual obligation is to the spouse and children, with the extended family second. A new family is formed. The previous takes a back seat. This is cleaving. We honour, and give weight, to all we have come from. We recognise the weight of both good and bad, and we make appropriate choices based on that weight. This is true honour, in order that we can move forward, in the blessing of God, for our future generations.

Jared and I sat together on a number of occasions in those early days, considering what our new home would be known for. We made lists from our families of origin, and from our prior marriage covenants, and we chose which things we would bring into our future, and which things we would leave behind. From a most painfully beautiful list, we prayerfully forged a new set of family values. Cleaving is a matter of honouring the past and the future simultaneously – both must co-exist.

This is a union between a man of valour, a fruitful vine and the Living Vine Himself. Marriage is a three-strand chord. Together they are the two becoming one in covenant with the Lord, a whole and perfect reflection of God in the Earth.

THE HEAD AND THE HEART

Our Lord is a God of order; He has already established an organisational pattern for all creation, including family. He has written the book of life and, in the books of the Bible, we can find all the answers for what is arguably life's most challenging role – that of the family.

Businesses use flow charts to determine the chain of command in a company, where the head of a business is the CEO, the president or director. From that point there are the executives, and departments, and various directors, and so on. It's a familiar flow chart.

Using this concept then, we can see easily that, seated at the top of the family flow chart, is and should always be the Lord Himself. God is the top of our family organisational flow chart – our family structure. He sets the standard. He sets the culture. He determines the behavioural patterns of the organisation, the family. How parents behave, and how children behave, is informed by the Lord. This should be evident in all Christian homes.

> *Therefore be imitators of God as dear children.*
> *Ephesians 5:1 (NKJV)*

For our own thriving we are to place God at the centre of our existence and so, naturally, at the centre of our homes also. The Lord is the head of the home, and sets the acceptable modes of operation. He establishes the values, the mission, the vision. The way we serve the community, the love we display to our neighbours, the way we exhibit good etiquette and manners. Our value for strong work ethic, and self-discipline, thriving marriages, and ordered finances. These are all beautiful agendas, governed by the Lord. It is a wise person who establishes these things by the ordinance, set by God, and laid out in Scripture.

The next tier of the family flow chart relates to the directors and, in the family, that is the husband and wife, the father and the mother. The two are side-by-side. The Bible teaches that marriage is a covenantal connection between a man and a woman, and is the most important human relationship in the family unit. These two become one flesh and, together, the perfect reflection of God. Together they are one. The marriage was initiated by God in the very beginning.

Established in the beginning, and to this day, marriage continues to be the foundation of both family and society. A successful family and home begins with putting God first, and then working to make sure the marriage relationship takes a place of prominence and leadership in the family unit. The greatest gift any parent could ever give their child is to have a strong life-giving, thriving marriage. This is why marriage has been under such attack. Husbands and wives must do all in their power to learn how to cultivate, and steward, heaven-centred, God-ordained, marriages. When we struggle to do this, it is not enough to say that our origins of broken homes discount us, or excuse us, from healthy marriages of our own into the future. We are empowered by the Word of God, and His Spirit, to live by His patterns. In Christ we are of a new blood line.

His desire for us is wholeness. We are overcomers. We may not be able to change our family history, but we surely can, and are mandated to, determine the future legacies that will come through us. We must make it our business to learn the ways of God in marriage. A successful family begins when God is first, and when the husband and wife work to make sure that their marriage relationship is healthy, and in a place of prominence, in the family unit.

The next tier of the flow chart is, of course, the children. It is the Lord's order that a child comes under the covering of their parents. It is the Lord's good grace that gives a child strength and covering, that is exercised in the authority of his or her parents. Essentially it is a child-parent relationship that teaches a child how to honour, and respect, authority in the future. Without learning this, a child will become an adult who will find it hard to honour the Lord. It is vitally important that we give our children the skill of understanding authority, the blessing of understanding authority, and the thriving that comes from submitting to covering. Our children will love and trust the Lord, if we teach them to love and to trust their parents in their formative years.

> *Children, obey your parents in the Lord, for this is right.*
> *Ephesians 6:1 (NKJV)*

Oh, it's easier said than done, isn't it? To teach your children to trust. It's a daily investment in relational equity. Daily building confidence, and walking in your authority in a way that teaches them safety and trust.

My youngest son, Jesse, is a strong-willed young man. He is the type of person who will adamantly insist on his point of view. When he decides on a matter there is absolutely no swaying him. As a mother, I recognise that this is an incredible asset, but it does present some significant challenges, as you can surely imagine.

When he was only 18 months old, he was playing with his three older siblings in a downstairs part of the house, while I was up in the bathroom preparing myself for the day. That was when I heard it – a bloodcurdling scream. Every mother knows the sound. Every mother also knows the difference between a cry that should be left to their own creative resolution without intervention, and that other type of cry that could mean an ambulance, or a trip to the hospital. This cry sounded like the latter.

I dropped everything and raced down the stairs. I was met with three wide-eyed, deadpan faces. Jesse was on the floor, sobbing by now. I could tell immediately his life was not in danger, but something quite traumatic had happened to him. I looked at his three siblings, and asked them what happened. To this day I do not know who was at fault but, on closer inspection, I noticed that my small boy was clutching his left hand. He was nursing what I would discover to be three chubby little fingers that had been flattened in the slamming of a door in its doorframe.

Those three little fingers bruised significantly, and he nursed them for days on end, not allowing anyone to come close to them. In the course of time, two of the fingernails came away and fell off. The third one stubbornly remained attached by just a tether. It was getting caught on his clothing, and getting in the way of his play. But he would not let anyone come close to it under any circumstances.

After I had enough of watching him trying to navigate this awkward scenario with his left hand, I brought him up to my bathroom, and sat him on the counter. I cupped his chubby little face with my palms and I asked him if he would let me cut the fingernail away. Although he couldn't speak very well at this tender age, he knew exactly what I was saying, and snatched his hand away, hiding it behind his back. A look of horror filled his eyes as he turned his face from mine. He could see the nail clippers on the bench beside him, and he started to squirm. I gently cupped his face again.

"Jesse, do you trust me?" I asked softly, with a deep compassion swelling in my heart riding on my words.

Almost as soon as the words left my mouth, I realised how foolish my question was, and how this could quickly backfire if he said no. But it was too late to change the proposition, and I had to wait for his response.

My eyes were locked with his, my hands around his cheeks. I quietly waited. His hazel eyes searched mine and, to my absolute surprise, he relaxed his shoulders and offered me his injured hand. He let me use the sharp metal instruments on that tiny little finger, and all was well. I'll always remember how precious that moment was, and how relieved I felt that he chose to trust me.

In essence, this is what we're trying to teach our children. That if they trust us, we can help them in the pains of life. We're trying to teach them that life will cause us injury from time to time and, even after we heal, some of the fallout may continue to cause us inconvenience and struggle. We're trying to teach them that they can trust our wisdom, even when it looks like a sharp metal instrument. We're trying to teach them that we know what is best for them. If we can do this, they will learn to trust God when they're grown and they've left our care. It is so important that our families understand the order that God has ordained in the home; for best flourishing.

We have an opportunity, and an urgency, to raise the question in our homes – who is setting the order and values of our family? Who is leading who?

In the culture of child-led families, we must remember that the greatest gift a parent can give their child is the stability of a loving relationship between husband and wife. When the child takes the lead, the family is out of order. The strength of the marital relationship is what brings the child a sense of security. Mum and Dad must put each other first, before the child. Children need to see their parents loving and prioritising one another, because that commitment brings order and security into the child's life, and into the family unit.

Parents must be careful not to invert the godly order of a home and a family. To do this is deeply harmful for both the child and the family. Often parents will allow this to happen out of fear. They genuinely fear losing their child's affection, and they allow the child to call the shots. However, a child who learns to get their way through defiance, tantrums, or charm, will be a child who will be unable to function well in school, or later in life. They would never actually have been required to learn self-regulation, and how to find their place in the world.

> *For Abraham will certainly become a great and mighty nation, and all the nations of the Earth will be blessed through him. I have singled him out so that he will direct his sons and their families to keep the way of the LORD by doing what is right and just. Then I will do for Abraham all that I have promised.*
>
> *Genesis 18:18-19 (NLT)*

When the Lord wanted a man to bring his nation through, he chose Abram (who was renamed Abraham). For the most part, the Lord chose Abraham in spite of his failures and human nature – this is the grace of God at work, and true of all of us. However, there is a single verse which describes why the Lord was predisposed to bring his people through Abraham's loins. In Genesis 18 verse 19, the Lord reveals that he was confident Abraham would be the one who would *teach his sons the ways of the Lord.* The Lord chose this man because he knew that he would be a teacher, and a leader. He was looking for a man who would not be led by culture, or the emotional demands of his own family. He was looking for a man who would lead the culture of Heaven into the nation.

> *My child, never forget the things I have taught you.*
> *Store my commands in your heart.*
> *If you do this, you will live many years,*
> *and your life will be satisfying.*
> *Proverbs 3:1-2 (NLT)*

And so we ask the question: who is leading our homes? We must question and redefine the child-led psychology in culture today. The child who grows up as the emotional, or practical centre, of the family's attention will have a distorted view of themselves and the world. That child also grows up under extreme pressure, self-imposed as well as allowed by their parents. This leadership weight is not for a child to carry.

Instead, a God-focused and marriage-centred home, where a child is loved deeply but understands that they are a part of something much larger, becomes a home that is secure. If a parent can honour the godly order of the family dynamic through their spiritual authority, consistency, and genuine care, their child will become a beautiful person.

Parents should continue prioritising intimacy, communication, and time together apart from the children, where they can connect, pray and strategise. A unified front between husband and wife, to uphold the standards of Heaven, is the very building block of a child's life.

The family is the first ministry of our lives. We are priests in the home. We are raising ministers of the Kingdom, who we can release one day into their generation. With the Lord at the head of the home, the husband and wife, in unity as a spiritual covering, can create an order for their children where they will thrive and grow.

Because healthy homes build healthy cities, and healthy cities impact culture.

SECTION TWO

Temple & Table

THE SACRED THRESHOLD

If you want to change the world, go home and love your family.

Mother Teresa

Over the course of the four generations since World War II, there has been an undeniable assault on the family. An intentional pressure to weaken marriage, and fragment the home. So much of the fracture we see in culture and society today, can be traced back to the breakdown of the family unit. We have slipped so far that we can barely even recognise it any more. What is normal today would have been absolutely shocking only generations ago.

While we try to put Band-Aids on social problems, with political policies and humanistic thought, things only continue to decline. As the world continues to turn its back on the Lord and His good wisdom, we see the tide of evil rise, resulting in a war against humanity itself. The family is the target, and the generations are in its wake.

Our marriages, our children, our families, have been dashed – sacrificed on altars built by the deceived and misled, generation after generation. Even in Christian homes, distractions and deceptions have eroded the strength that families once offered to society. Husbands and wives have forsaken their God-ordained roles in the family, and turned against each other. Children are left without leadership, covering, refuge, and identity. Single parent homes are commonplace in our time. Children and adolescents are handed over to daycare care centres, schools, sporting clubs, and hobbies.

> *God says, "I'm rebuking you parents for not letting your children burn." We're losing thousands and thousands of kids because we wanted them to be successful rather than burning. You want them to get an education? You send them to a university and turn them over to the professors of Babylon. Is it any wonder they come back and they're living alternative lifestyles? Why would you turn your children to be discipled by pagans? I wouldn't send my Daniel anywhere to a university unless he was prepared like Daniel, to challenge the Babylon universities.*
>
> *Lou Engle*

Lives are full to the brim, but void of the Spirit, and void of connection with the spiritual guardians who give the greatest sense of purpose, meaning, and identity. Strangers are raising our kids. Through surrogate guardians, the anti-Kingdom agenda of the age is shaping their ideologies. Parents have abdicated the roles of leader, teacher, coach, counsellor, and priest. With each passing generation, the fallout is greater.

Busy careers and schedules are denying children the opportunity to build formative bonds with their mothers and fathers, creating deep deficits in their souls. They grow to be children who cannot give or receive social information. They cannot function in a social world; they have no healthy grid for interaction, connection, or the giving and receiving of love. They are numb. They have little regard or care for others. They are surrounded by people, and yet unable to connect. They have been rushed out of the home at an early age, in the early hours, brought back late and entertained by devices, all the while never a genuine connection made between mother and child, father and child.

Our children, the costly sacrifices on the altars of career, sexuality, pride, materialism, and self. All a plight of humankind's constant warring enemy. His tactics, while not at all subtle, have been relentless over the decades of recent history.

> *For we do not wrestle against flesh and blood, but against the rulers, against the authorities, against the cosmic powers over this present darkness, against the spiritual forces of evil in the heavenly places.*
> *Ephesians 6:12 (ESV)*

The world is looking to political structures, and social justice programs, to fix what they will never be able to fix. This is a spiritual problem. We have wandered too far from the truth. We have tried and failed at making truth relative – subject to preferences and emotion. We've replaced the Word of God with worldly psychology, and we are wondering why things are in the dire condition they are. But the Bible told us these days would come, and it should be no surprise.

> *But understand this, that in the last days there will come times of difficulty. For people will be lovers of self, lovers of money, proud, arrogant, abusive, disobedient to their parents, ungrateful, unholy, heartless, unappeasable, slanderous, without self-control, brutal, not loving good, treacherous, reckless, swollen with conceit, lovers of pleasure rather than lovers of God, having the appearance of godliness, but denying its power. Avoid such people. For among them are those who creep into households and capture weak women, burdened with sins and led astray by various passions, always learning and never able to arrive at a knowledge of the truth.*
> *2 Timothy 3:1-7 (ESV)*

We truly are living in those days. Ironically, we have elevated 'self' at the expense of ourselves. It was Saint Basil who said, "Hell can't be made attractive, so the devil makes attractive the road that leads there." So very true and, sadly, society is a case in point.

But I can see an awakening stirring in the generation today. And I am grateful that the Lord, is His kindness and wisdom, has not hidden from us the dynamic design for family, which is, in turn, the dynamic design for healthy cities and nations – and the dynamic design for entire generations. It all starts in the fundamental building block of the family unit. For me it starts at what I've come to call the Temple and Table of the Family Altar. This is where worship begins, and where our truest selves are fashioned.

Resifiant Humans

It is hard work being a teenager in a world full of temptations, discoveries, conflict, and crisis. It's hard when you don't know yourself yet, and your senses and emotions are still maturing. But that is the whole point. That is the training ground – because there is only one thing harder than being a teenager, and that is being an adult. When the buck stops with you, and there is no parental net to fall into any longer. So a parent's job is to socialise and train the young person for the wide world. The kindest thing a parent can do is teach the young person who they are to be in the midst of the wind and the fire.

Rather than rescue, we coach. Rather than bail, we build. It wasn't long ago that virtues, like endurance, commitment, hard work, and grit, were aspirational and admired. Entitlement was the antithesis of sacrifice. Escapism was the antithesis of courage. Convenience was the antithesis of selflessness. Retreat was the antithesis of connection. Self was the opposite of love.

A godly home builds resilient humans who can face the world with eyes set like flint, engaged and compassionate hearts, sharp minds, and broad shoulders. Every child has a genius of Heaven wrapped up inside them. Mothers must train; fathers must set the standard.

The need is great in the world today. The seed of hope is in our children, and we must teach them to do hard things. We must teach them that fear is not an option. We must teach them that courage outweighs fear, and the turbulent world needs them to live by conviction rather than convenience, and mission rather than mood. We must teach them that, if they don't rise, a whole generation will miss out.

This learning starts younger than you would imagine. These skills are taught and learned from day one. As parents, we must have this revelation preceding the moment of their birth. We are not raising children. We are raising adults. With that end in mind, we can clearly define the type of coaching required through early childhood, and into the adolescent years. It is simultaneously a beautiful privilege and a sobering responsibility.

> *I do not pray that You should take them out of the world, but that You should keep them from the evil one. They are not of the world, just as I am not of the world. Sanctify them by Your truth. Your word is truth. As You sent Me into the world, I also have sent them into the world.*
>
> *John 17:15-18 (NKJV)*

It starts in an environment where healthy boundaries are established early. Where children know what is acceptable, and unacceptable, behaviour. And how are they to learn this? Through discipline and consequence, as well as reward and celebration.

Parenting is a relentless task of consistency. We must pick our battles wisely and, once chosen, we must remain resolute until the lesson is learned and life-giving. We should beware never to pick battles that we will not harness the endurance to see through. The child will gain a great sense of security knowing that their parents are consistent and stable. Once a value has been embraced, it must be pursued until it is deeply imprinted – becoming like a well from which they can draw for a lifetime.

It is likely your child will initially push back on those boundaries. Not because the boundary is oppressive, but because the child wants to know how secure and important it really is. Once the boundary is established, the child finds security and identity within it. The trouble is, I see too many parents who lack the fortitude to discern where the boundary should be set. Many also lack the fortitude to see the lesson through. It's dangerous when a child pushes back, and is allowed to overrun and defy a value that would, one-day, serve them to their benefit, and to the benefit of the generation they are called to.

Children can learn social rules and limits early in life. If a parent tolerates behaviours that are unacceptable, that child eventually develops beneath their potential. They also develop habits that will be socially challenging in their future relationships, professionally and personally. We do our children an incredible favour when we teach them appropriate social etiquette. This is the mandate of parenting.

Discipline and boundary-setting is an act of ultimate love for the future well-being and excellence of our children. We cannot avoid discipline because of fear, guilt and misplaced empathy. The writer of Proverbs implores his son not to despise the discipline of the Lord, clearly stating that the Lord disciplines the ones He loves, just as a father does to his son who he has high hopes for.

> *My son, do not despise the LORD's discipline*
> *or be weary of His reproof,*
> *for the LORD reproves him whom He loves,*
> *as a father the son in whom he delights.*
> *Proverbs 3:11-12 (ESV)*

We discipline, not because we are disappointed with our children. We discipline because we love them, and we long to see the manifestation of the potential within them. When they behave in ways beneath the excellence they carry, we hold them to account for it.

To avoid discipline is unkind, because the child has then been denied the lessons needed for self-regulation. It is destructive because it leaves children unprepared to face the world. It is unkind because it produces people who are self-centred, and inconsiderate of how their behaviours impact the world around them. Ultimately these people will struggle in their adult lives.

The most empathetic thing you can do is to provide safe parameters for your child to learn within. Your child craves your leadership more than your friendship. Remarkably, leadership becomes the very foundation for intimate friendship. It does not work the other way around.

Our children often joke that we are the strictest parents they know. They laugh because, deep down, they are grateful. They often express genuine thanks. These conversations take on a more serious tone, sometimes sounding like, "Mum, I'm so grateful for what you taught me. I can see how some of my friends are making choices that are hurting them, and it's really sad to watch."

Please hear me – this is not about being a perfect parent, or raising perfect children. I am simply speaking from Scripture, and from experience, as a parent who seeks to guide their children toward the excellence God has placed within them. When I speak of a child's excellence, I'm not referring to career success, or performance, but to the core of who they are – the person they are becoming in the world. Will they grow to be decent, compassionate human beings, who serve God with their whole hearts? This, I believe, is the true mandate of parenting.

Beyond Manners

Basic behavioural standards supersede personality profiles, social status, or privilege. The type of etiquette that displays who a person is at their core. A type of etiquette that displays the value they hold for the people around them. Common kindness, warmth, hospitality, and service.

In our home, we set nine table settings every day. It is hilarious. I smile almost every time I lay out all those plates. We often comment about how it's a youth camp every day in our house. I know I will miss those nine plates one day, and the effort required to fill them all. If you haven't already thought of it, I can assure you that it is impossible to please nine individual palettes and preferences. Two in our family dislike pumpkin and sweet potato, four don't like prawns, three prefer heavy spice, all but one dislikes quinoa, one doesn't like gnocchi, another prefers not to eat pesto, it's a split vote between brown rice and white rice, and I could go on and on. But at our table, everyone is served the same meal and we live under the mantra that says 'fussiness is rudeness'. We quietly determined to raise children who were politely grateful for the efforts made for their meals. We were determined to broaden their eating habits into sophisticated well-rounded palettes, where appreciation and enjoyment was always at the forefront of their minds.

There are aspects of social etiquette that go beyond personality. Whether a child is naturally introverted or extroverted, they can be taught the social skills that help them become likeable and considerate members of society. Often without realizing it, parents can unintentionally teach children to place themselves at the centre of the world's orbit, rather than teaching them how they come across, or guiding them to act in selfless, hospitable, and generous ways.

Sometimes parents excuse their children from upholding social standards because 'they are shy', 'a little distracted', or 'free-spirited'. In doing so, we teach our children to enter social settings focused on what they will gain, rather than what they can contribute or learn. We miss the opportunity to teach them emotional intelligence (EQ) and, in the process, we risk raising children who are more self-focused than curious, grateful and engaged.

Recently I took our daughter, Layla, for a 17th birthday shopping spree into the centre of town. As she was in a change room, I took my seat on a couch in the nearby waiting space. A young woman sat beside me on the three-seater couch. She had her earphones in, and she was on a phone call. She was obviously comfortable with the fact that everyone in that change room could hear the whole topic of her conversation. She was loudly describing, to the person on the other end of the call, about her disappointment in a particular relationship. Clearly this relationship was not meeting her needs and her expectations. She was adamantly describing how she would, and would not, be treated by this person. She was cursing without restraint, while describing intimate details that really should have remained private. After a couple of minutes, she identified the person on the other end of the call as her mother! My heart sank. Not a peer or a friend of a similar age. This was her mother encouraging her, in this vulgar and egocentric approach, to relationships. Clearly, the blind leading the blind down a spiral path.

On the drive home, I asked Layla whether she heard the girl on the phone in the change room. Layla nodded – she had heard. We discussed what it was about the conversation which made us so grieved. Eventually we realised it was because we now live in a culture where we have placed ourselves at the centre. We quickly reflected on the central message of the gospel – to lay down one's self for another.

> *But whoever desires to become great among you, let him be your servant. And whoever desires to be first among you, let him be your slave – just as the Son of Man did not come to be served, but to serve, and to give His life a ransom for many.*
>
> *Matthew 20:26-28 (NKJV)*

Layla and I talked about how far the world has strayed from that moral reality. Today we live in a culture with almost the opposite goal. The gospel of our day is self-focused – everyone else should lay down their lives for me, and I must fight for whatever I feel entitled to.

> *But know this, that in the last days perilous times will come: For men will be lovers of themselves, lovers of money, boasters, proud, blasphemers, disobedient to parents, unthankful, unholy, unloving, unforgiving,*

slanderers, without self-control, brutal, despisers of good, traitors, headstrong, haughty, lovers of pleasure rather than lovers of God, having a form of godliness but denying its power. And from such people turn away!
2 Timothy 3:1-5 (NKJV)

What ever happened to just being kind, polite, gentle, selfless? What does it look like to raise godly children in this environment?

I quickly remember it was the same child, Layla, who, for a period of time, would tantrum at the childcare gate each morning. In prayer, I asked God to help me understand what was happening for her and how I could lead her through it. I remember having a conversation with Layla, as a three-year-old, about the plans and purposes of God for her within that classroom. Our approach changed. We began talking to her about the answer she could be to her friends, and her teachers. We began sending her to daycare on a mission. Her demeanour began to change. She was beginning to look for opportunities to be an answer, to bring joy, to serve, and to make others feel better.

One particular day, when I was picking her up from daycare, her teacher quietly pulled me to the side. Mrs Amy was her name, and she was in her second trimester of pregnancy.

"Karolina, I have to tell you about something that happened a couple of weeks ago," she said. "We were sitting on the floor as the class was feeling the baby move in my belly. When it came time for me to stand again, I expressed the pain that I had been nursing in my back for a number of months. Layla stopped me and the class, and suggested that the children all gather around me to pray for my healing. Karolina, the pain left and hasn't returned in the two weeks since."

We need to teach our children that the world is not about them. We need to teach them to live lives where their own flesh is crucified daily, and their lives are lived in the awareness, love and service of others. We must teach them the golden rules – love God and love others.

Jesus replied, "'You must love the Lord *your God with all your heart, all your soul, and all your mind.' This is the first and greatest commandment. A second is equally important: 'Love your neighbour as yourself.' The entire law and all the demands of the prophets are based on these two commandments."*
Matthew 22:37-40 (NLT)

In our family we adopted the term 'Where's Wally' for their everyday exploits. Perhaps you're familiar with the childhood *Where's Wally* books. Each page is a busy explosion of colour and crowd. The purpose of each new page is to find one hidden figure, a man named Wally with a red and white striped shirt, glasses and beanie. He is sneakily hidden within the chaotic nature of each crowded page. And once he has been found, the mission of that page has been accomplished – only to turn to the next page for a new picture and a new search. The search for Wally begins again.

I wondered, as a young mum, how to break my children out of their fleshly tendency to care predominantly for themselves as they wandered off into the schoolyard each day. One day at home, as I watched one of my children look through a *Where's Wally* book, it dawned on me. The next morning as we were preparing for school, I told the kids that today, at school, they would be looking for Wally. They all looked up at me intrigued.

"Today, the Wally in your school might be someone who is sad or alone, or who has forgotten their lunch. It could be someone who is being bullied or overlooked. It might even be your teacher, looking overwhelmed and in need of help. You are going to look for Wally today because God is sending you into your school to be an answer. You will look for a need, and step in to meet it. You will seek opportunities to show the love of Jesus, doing it as an act of worship, knowing that He is using you to bless those around you. The only rule is this – it must be someone you don't know at all, or someone you wouldn't normally reach out to."

One afternoon, our youngest daughter, Korah, leapt into the car, beaming with excitement. "Mum!" she exclaimed, "I found my Wally today!" She went on to describe a young girl in the playground, sitting alone and visibly upset. Korah had gone over, gently befriended her, and watched as the little girl's face lit up with a smile. She even remembered her name as she told us the story – a remarkable first, since Korah rarely remembers other children's names. This particular girl had clearly made an impression on her heart. Right before my eyes, I witnessed our normally hesitant, and shy, five-year-old discovering the joy and purpose of serving.

We can and must teach them to deny self-gratification, and to live generously towards God and others. When our children make displays of resistance, or even fear, we remember that the core issue is a desire to satisfy self. Fear and rebellion are selfish acts. How incredibly inspiring to raise adults who can rise above their own desires for gratification and self. Oh, what a call. My heart stirs towards that end every day.

SPIRITUAL GIANTS

The two greatest influences in a person's formation are their family of origin, and the spiritual worldview they adopt. Let us not be mistaken in thinking that an agnostic or atheist family is devoid of spiritual influence. In reality, in the absence of a Christian foundation, a child will be discipled by the world. The spiritual worldview of a family, that identifies as agnostic or atheistic is, in effect, aligned with the spirit of the world. We can be certain that this discipleship is dynamic, forceful, and clear. This brings us back to the central truth – a person's formation is shaped by their family of origin, and the spiritual perspective held by that family. No family is perfect; every family carries generational patterns and mindsets that must either be nurtured and reinforced, or identified and corrected.

Particularly in the family dynamic, a child is formed and shaped through the interactions and experiences of the collective whole. Their place in the family adds light and shade to the rich experiences they will have on a larger scale as adults outside the home. The foundational learnings they receive in a healthy family environment are rich deposits.

> *It takes a combination of faith and works, success and struggles, failure and fortitude to produce the kind of success that becomes a legacy to be passed on to our children. It is not always what we leave to them as how much we leave in them.*
>
> *TD Jakes*

It's in the context of family that a child learns the deep foundations in the character and nature of the Lord. The child will watch the family navigate joys and struggles. The child will learn the nature of God by the way the family responds to circumstances.

Is this a mighty God who can be trusted? Are my interactions with Him, and the world, of eternal significance? Does the gospel have bearing in my life?

We will not hide these truths from our children;
we will tell the next generation
about the glorious deeds of the Lord,
about His power and His mighty wonders.
So each generation should set its hope anew on God,
not forgetting His glorious miracles
and obeying His commands.
Psalm 78: 4 & 7 (NLT)

A dynamic influence of spiritual formation is the spiritual community that the individual exists within. There is an urgency in our day for families to prioritise Church commitment. The greatest gift I can give my children is exposure to the glory of God – regular encounters where they can experience Him, for themselves, in an undeniable way. The deceptive call of the current day isolates people and families from Church communities. Persuasive arguments have convinced people that Church connection is not essential. The Church community is falling further down the list of priorities in our families today, and the next generation are the casualties.

The Church exists for nothing else but to draw Man into Christ to make them little Christ. If they're not doing that then all the cathedrals, clergy, missions, sermons and even the Bible itself are simply a waste of time. God became man for no other purpose.

CS Lewis

It's the repetition in the spiritual environments where saints gather for worship, prayer, and teaching of the Word, that creates opportunities for a person to catch the flame. While it is not the exclusive means, connection in corporate worship is certainly a dynamic one. We bring our children into the House of God, and we position them around the community of God's people regularly enough so that they will have every opportunity to have an encounter with God themselves.

We see this in Scripture, with Samuel in the temple (1 Samuel 3). This young man had been dedicated to the Lord's service as a baby by his mother. As a young child she brought him to the temple for full-time service. Yet it wasn't until his adolescent years when he finally had an encounter with God himself – an encounter he would recognise as such. It took years for the young man to recognise the presence of God.

I have seen this in the life of my own children. Born as pastor's kids, they have sat through more services than I could ever try to count, a minimum of three every Sunday from birth. My son, Judah, a beautiful, sweet, mild-tempered young man, was 13 when he encountered God in a life-changing way. That encounter sparked the awakening in him that I had prayed for his whole life. The young man, who came alive in a corporate worship setting, has exceeded my hopes as a mother. He hears and sees from his Saviour, maintains a thriving prayer and devotional life, and has picked up the guitar to join the worship team. Thirteen years of consistent connection to the House of God, and God's people, laid the foundation, and over time the routine became revelation in his own spirit.

> *I feel sorry for the children whose parents let them choose when they attend Church. They miss out on the discipline of doing the right thing when it feels good and when it does not and most of all they lose out on the exposure to an atmosphere that helps them construct an internal value system where the spirit man becomes trained.*
>
> *Bill Johnson*

The fruit of planting family in a Church community, and including corporate worship as a priority, is exponentially greater than we could ever anticipate. At the time of writing this I've been in Church pastoral ministry for more than 25 years – 14 of those years were with teenagers and families, and 12 years now as the lead pastor of a Church congregation. I have been doing this for a long time. Please trust me when I tell you that I have seen a direct correlation between a family's Church connection in attendance and serving, and the future adult child's faith.

> *You can only teach what you know, but you reproduce who you are.*
> *John C Maxwell*

It takes more than the lip service of a parent's confession of faith. It takes even more than the genuine core beliefs a parent may hold. Example is paramount. What we prioritise, in our actions and allocation of time, not just in our words or hopes, is what teaches the next generation. As the saying goes, what walks in the father runs in the son.

There are always exceptions. I readily admit that I have seen faithful families, committed and connected in the Church community, believing for years for the return of a prodigal child. There are reasons these situations occur. Sometimes, although not always, those children have been exposed to words or experiences in the home where hurt has cast a negative light on God, Church members, or Church leadership. We must be careful how we process our own experiences in front of our children, and equally careful how we process their experiences with them.

On the other hand, I have also seen exceptional, passionate young followers of Christ, who come from non-committed, or spiritually adverse families. Often these young people attribute their faith to a praying relative, a friend, a chaplain, or a youth leader, who provided a positive example, and a guiding influence for them to follow.

There are warning signs and statements that I've heard over nearly three decades – variations of justified reasoning to lessen the importance of Church connection for the family. Well-meaning Christians promise that they'll return in the off-season, when sport isn't taking place on Sundays anymore. Or that the family budget required that extra work hours be made on a Sunday. I've even heard families comment that they want to keep Sundays for family time after a busy week. My heart aches.

After much prayer, I believe the Spirit of God revealed to me that many people approach the Church out of *principle rather than revelation.* Anything we do out of principle will eventually become an obligation, at the risk of becoming a begrudging offering. But that which is birthed, out of revelation, is the source of life-giving joy. A principle is simply law, and law has no life in it. But revelation, born of the Spirit, carries a grace which brings about joy and life-giving fruit.

> *So He (Jesus) came to Nazareth where He had been brought up and as his custom was He went into the synagogue on the Sabbath day and stood up to read.*
> *Luke 14:16 (NIV)*

If it was Jesus' custom, then it should be ours also. I personally have deep joy encouraging a person to locate themselves, and their family, in the House of God as a *weekly* priority, because I personally know the impact it has had on my own life, and my family. It has changed my life. It has anchored my soul. It has filled my lungs with new breath, time and time again. I have sat under the weight of glory. I've heard the Spirit's whispers. I have cultivated lifelong relationships. I've broken mindsets, and learned new ways of living. Where else would I be? Where else could be more valuable?

There used to be a time when families prioritised the House of God every week. Where culture had a Biblical world view, and everything else fell around, and after, the gathering of the Saints. Businesses closed down, and worship took precedence. Participation in corporate worship was the non-negotiable of the week. Parents led their families into the House of God.

When God is at the top of the structure of my life, when His worship and commitment to His body is my first priority, then I am placing the highest values first. When I do this as a value for family – this *is* family time. My child's connection to a sports team, or a casual workplace, will not give them the spiritual foundation they will need in life. Family time includes the House of God together. Rest begins in the place of His worship; and not only do we attend, but we serve that community as well.

Teaching our children to serve is possibly one of the most countercultural things we can teach them. I can honestly say that the reason our seven, grieving children, have come through their loss with strength is partly due to their posture of mission, and serving in the House of God. We are on mission together, and we turn ourselves outward, even when – especially when – life is trying to turn us inward.

What a privilege to help them rise beyond the commodity-driven, self-serving, consumer culture, that their peers are being swallowed up in. To raise young people who know what it is to give their lives away for others in the household of faith – how truly beautiful.

We learn, in Proverbs 31, the light starts in the home. And that bright lamp is meant to burn through all the seasons, and all the nights. It's the lamp that burns at home which allows a family to laugh, and have joy as it looks into the future without fear.

Who can find a virtuous wife?
For her worth is far above rubies.
The heart of her husband safely trusts her;
So he will have no lack of gain.
She does him good and not evil
All the days of her life.
She seeks wool and flax,

And willingly works with her hands.
She is like the merchant ships,
She brings her food from afar.
She also rises while it is yet night,
And provides food for her household,
And a portion for her maidservants.
She considers a field and buys it;
From her profits she plants a vineyard.
She girds herself with strength,
And strengthens her arms.
She perceives that her merchandise is good,
And her lamp does not go out by night.
She stretches out her hands to the distaff,
And her hand holds the spindle.
She extends her hand to the poor,
Yes, she reaches out her hands to the needy.
She is not afraid of snow for her household,
For all her household is clothed with scarlet.
She makes tapestry for herself;
Her clothing is fine linen and purple.
Her husband is known in the gates,
When he sits among the elders of the land.
She makes linen garments and sells them,
And supplies sashes for the merchants.
Strength and honour are her clothing;
She shall rejoice in time to come.
She opens her mouth with wisdom,
And on her tongue is the law of kindness.
She watches over the ways of her household,
And does not eat the bread of idleness.
Her children rise up and call her blessed;
Her husband also, and he praises her:

"Many daughters have done well,
But you excel them all."
Charm is deceitful and beauty is passing,
But a woman who fears the LORD, she shall be praised.
Give her of the fruit of her hands,
And let her own works praise her in the gates.
Proverbs 31: 10-31 (NKJV)

It's a lamp that burns at home which produces fruitfulness and good testimony. It's the lamp that burns at home which ministers in the marketplace and at the city gates of governmental influence. We have to turn up the light, and it starts in the home.

It's in the family that we raise Spiritual Giants. A child's spiritual condition in the home will determine who they become as an adult. We cannot leave it up to a child to decide when they're ready. Relating to spiritual matters, oftentimes it's the lack of guidance in childhood that inadvertently teaches a child that spirituality is simply not even important. This philosophical and humanistic line of reasoning does an extreme disservice to a child in the long run. The truth, is as Christian parents we owe our children an encounter with God.

> *Now therefore, fear the LORD, serve Him in sincerity and in truth, and put away the gods which your fathers served on the other side of the River and in Egypt. Serve the LORD! And if it seems evil to you to serve the LORD, choose for yourselves this day whom you will serve, whether the gods which your fathers served that were on the other side of the River, or the gods of the Amorites, in whose land you dwell.* ***But as for me and my house, we will serve the LORD.***
>
> *Joshua 24:14-15 (NKJV)*

GUARDING THE GATES

As I've said earlier, my upbringing didn't offer me a worldview that was conducive to ministry. I had a traditional Catholic cultural background, but my experience of Christianity was very separate and compartmentalised, away from the lived experience of everyday life. As I became a mother, I was endlessly in pursuit of keys and tools, to help raise my children in a passionate experience of God.

On one particular weekend we were hosting a large youth event, and had invited a guest to minister. This woman was someone who I had looked up to from a distance. I considered it a great privilege to be able to spend a couple of days with her, as she ministered in our Church.

On one of the car trips between events, I asked her how to facilitate an environment where my children would become hungry for the things of God. Her answer was simple and profound.

"They need an encounter of their own."

She taught me not to assume that, just because my children were the children of pastors, that they would know God by default.

"Practice it at home," she told me. "Create moments where you teach them to pray. Teach them to hear the voice of God. Teach them to prophesy. Teach them how to pray for others."

She taught me that, if I could create environments at home where my children could have an encounter with God for themselves, they would be able to hold their own out in the wider world. The private experiences at home would birth, within them, an undeniable unshakeable faith of their own.

It was some of the best advice I have ever received, even to this day. And I have applied it. I confess, at first it was awkward. But only until it was not awkward anymore. My children did start to hear the voice of God. They did start to encounter Him. Their ears began to tune in to Heaven's frequency. They grew in boldness and confidence. They began to pray for their friends at school, and travel with me on ministry trips where they would prophesy and release healing in auditoriums.

We teach them the skills in the Spirit realm. We teach them how to discover, and practice, their unique Spiritual gifts. We teach them to hear from God. We teach them to act in obedience to His promptings. We read Scripture with them. We prophesy destiny over them.

Moses and David, though hundreds of years apart, were both adamant about what was allowed in and out of the temple – into the Holy Place, in the presence of the Lord. Gatekeepers and priests were charged with the responsibility of making sure that the atmosphere was protected, and would remain clean and reverent. The same must be true of our homes.

As parents we are the gatekeepers. It is obvious that we wouldn't allow a thief, or a violent person, through the front door of our home. Yet so many of us allow destructive things into the atmosphere of our homes, through movies, television shows, and music. The content that streams into our homes, through these gates, is filled with violence and compromise. The culture of the world, and demoralising forces, are rushing into our homes, and into the hearts of our children, through gateways which are wide open and unprotected.

The rates of online content consumption for children and teenagers is continually rising and, with the introduction of artificial intelligence, we are quickly learning that young people are using devices and online platforms for relational connection. The upcoming generation is suffering from loneliness, which they are remedying by using bots for friendship and connection. The statistics and the stories of the effects of this grooming are horrific.

Social media is discipling our children every day, for multiple hours on end. Algorithms are targeting their desires based on click-behaviour, and the reactions they make as they interact online. The content of music and streaming services is unguarded and limitless. Parents are mostly unaware, and largely distracted by the busyness of their own lives.

Even the themes of childhood movies are contrary to the standards of Heaven, subtly but relentlessly eroding the core foundations of our faith as Christians. Personally, I don't have a problem with Disney or Pixar. A device, or a screen in itself, is mostly neutral in its nature. But what I do find conflicting is an upbringing where a child can more easily quote movie scripts than Scripture, Disney plots more readily than Bible stories, are more familiar with entertainment culture than prayer or the presence of God.

While we may employ the vehicles of media for rest and downtime, we must also recognise them as gates, doors, and entry points for the culture of our homes. In our resting, and our celebrating at the altar of family, we must guard the atmosphere. This means monitoring what comes into the sanctuary of the spaces that should be the safest, purest and strongest of places. We not only guard, but we coach as well. We teach our children, and our young people, about the temple of their own hearts, and what is required for those temples to remain pure and holy, and consecrated to the Lord.

We teach our young people how quickly and easily those spaces can get polluted. We teach them how to stand in the face of countercultural influences. We teach them how to discern between good and evil. We create regular environments, where candid conversation can take place so that we have an understanding of the world in which our children live. We want to pick up on subtle cues, and lovingly guide with full awareness and discernment. We bring correction and perspective where it's needed without delay.

Ordinary Hands, Extraordinary Deeds

I remember when my oldest daughter, and her cohorts, were each allocated an electronic device by the Christian school our children attended. Parents were offered an iPad safety seminar on a weekday evening, where we could come and learn about the dangers of electronic devices and online behaviour. They would also disclose, and teach, about the precautionary measures they had taken on each device assigned to the students. I attended the seminar, and I brought my daughter with me. She was only 12 years old at the time, and she was the only child there that night. When she asked me why I insisted on her coming, I told her it was because I wanted her to know all the things that I had been taught. So that we could have full disclosure and transparency before one another, as we entered this online space together as a family.

A great sense of overwhelm washed over me that night, as I listened to the content that was being delivered to a room full of Gen X and Millennial parents. I realised that we really have no idea what our children get up to online, and how savvy they are in that virtual space. In the car on the way home, I quietly confessed to Maja, "I feel helpless to be able to protect you." Her response marked me. "Mum, I guess you'll have to trust me."

When she said that, I flashed back to an event, several years prior, when I was sitting on the front row of a conference hearing a family counsellor give a keynote address. She had been asked to speak around issues regarding online safety. Although I was in the House of the Lord, a place of worship with the family of believers, the spirit of fear and dread still assaulted me at that moment. I cried out in my heart, "Lord, spare my children. Help me."

Immediately the Holy Spirit whisper deep into my soul. "I will make the Sun stand still for you on the day when the battle comes to your door. I will give you the time and space to fix the situation before it gets dark." (Joshua 10:12-14) I've held on to that promise for almost two decades, and I've seen the Hand of God bring this promise to pass, time and time again in our family.

Isn't that just the truth about our parenting? To be the best stewards we can be, fully engaged as coaches and guides, with the goal of raising responsible trustworthy and Christ-centred adults – we lean entirely on the Lord, knowing that ultimately we cannot do this alone. They are His children, our entrustment, for His plans in the Earth. He has a vested interest in their prospering. He will enable us for the task.

We can only use what is in our possession to carry out this role. The Lord does not expect any more of us, though He certainly doesn't expect anything less. The enemy is coming to our door. He is brazen. In our current culture, he doesn't even bother disguising himself any more. He is shameful, unabashed, and appalling. He comes brazenly through the gateways and doors of our homes. It is entirely up to us to guard those doors, to destroy him, to protect the purity of our homes and our families from his presence.

> *For who is powerful enough to enter the house of a strong man and plunder his goods? Only someone even stronger – someone who could tie him up and then plunder his house.*
>
> *Matthew 12:29 (NLT)*

Our enemy presents himself as a strong man, but there is One stronger still, whose leading in our homes is supreme if we surrender to His guidance. Our weapons are Spiritual ones, and the One within us is greater than the one in the world (1 John 4:4).

I take heart from Jael's story in Judges chapter 4.

> *But Sisera fled away on foot to the tent of Jael, the wife of Heber the Kenite... And Jael came out to meet Sisera and said to him, "Turn aside, my lord; turn aside to me; do not be afraid." So he turned aside to her into the tent, and she covered him with a rug. And he said to her, "Please give me a little water to drink, for I am thirsty." So she opened a skin of milk and gave him a drink and covered him. And he said to her, "Stand at the opening of the tent, and if any man comes and asks you,*

'Is anyone here?' say, 'No.'" But Jael, the wife of Heber, took a tent peg, and took a hammer in her hand. Then she went softly to him and drove the peg into his temple until it went down into the ground while he was lying fast asleep from weariness. So he died.

Judges 4:17-21 (ESV)

Deborah and Barak were leading the army of the nation of God in a war against the Canaanite army. Sisera was the commander of the Canaanite army. When he saw that his troops were beginning to fall, this despicable coward fled for his life. He left his men to die, and sought to save himself.

In those days, men and women often lived in separate dwellings, and it was entirely inappropriate for a man to present himself at the door of a woman's tent. Sisera's behaviour in this passage is shameful. Not only did he approach Jael in her private tent, but he also asked a woman to protect him.

I consider this in light of all the evils that brazenly greet our families. Commanders of the enemy's armies march up to the doors of our lives. Often our initial feelings might have been similar to Jael's shock and confusion. I have felt times of fear, dread, and have felt overwhelmed. This would have been the shock that Jael felt when she saw Sisera's face at the door of her tent. But, in the split second she had to react, she disallowed fear and turned the moment into an opportunity. She acted. She gave him much more than what he asked for.

This physical and natural strength of the enemy at her door was far greater than her training and ability. She might not have been good with a sword or a javelin, but she knew how to use a tent peg to secure her home. She knew that the milk she had cultivated would prove medicinal in a life-threatening situation. Given her tenacity and cunning courage, he was no match for her. She used what she had with boldness and skill. She was confident in the home she had built. She would take down a vicious enemy commander. Physically, she was overpowered, but Spiritually she had the upper hand.

These are the homes we build and protect. We do all this in a victorious, resolute, strategic manner. Any enemy should come to regret the assumptions made when appearing at our thresholds.

In the lives of our families, our presence should instil confidence rather than weariness. Too many Christian parents hover over their children out of a sense of fear. The result is a generation of young people who don't know how to hold their own in a hostile world, a world that is opposed to God. They've been taught to hide and protect themselves, rather than to lead and counteract.

If you faint in the day of adversity,
Your strength is small.
Proverbs 24:10 (NKJV)

Not Jael. Her job was, and our job is, to be strong and resolute. So strong, that resolute young people can be built in the next generation. A generation who knows their God, and who will do great exploits for Him. Our job is not to cower before an enemy, but to take him out. By our example we must teach the next generation how to set their faces like flint in the face of their environments, distinguishing what each occasion demands for Kingdom influence.

The spirit of the age would have us hiding, trying to protect and cover ourselves, and the ones we love. But this is not the way of the victorious Christ follower. This is not the model Jesus, or the Bible heroes, gave us. We are called to stand in the midst of the darkness, and tell a loud and resounding story that counters the narrative.

We have a different story to boldly tell the world. The story that every generation aches to hear. Announcing the acceptable year of the Lord is the declaration that rides in on the back of every believing generation. We must teach our children what that story is, and how to tell it without fear. There is only one way to do this – by laying the right foundations deep within their beings, by discipling them in the things of God, in ways that far outweigh the discipleship they receive in the world. We determine the atmosphere of our homes, and our families.

We teach them the Word of God – His precepts, His character, His ways, His nature, His name, His promises. They must be familiar with His Word if they are going to be able to run well in a world filled with stumbling blocks. They must know who He is if they're going to have any chance of leading courageous lives of Kingdom purpose.

> *Great peace have those who love Your law,*
> *And nothing causes them to stumble.*
> *Psalm 119:165 (NKJV)*

> *How can a young person stay pure?*
> *By obeying your word.*
> *Psalm 119:9 (NLT)*

Where does the Word of God fall on your list of priorities as a family? Do your children see you, with your spouse, in the Scriptures in the quiet hours of the day? Do your children have their own personal times in the Word every day? Do your little ones sit under the sound of your voice as you read Scripture to them? What is the code they're learning? Is it the Kingdom of Heaven, or is it the world?

We are to set atmospheres in our homes, where the Word is truly like daily bread. Where prayer is a familiar sound, and worship spills out spontaneously and intentionally all through the week. We cannot abdicate the responsibility of discipleship to a screen, a school, culture, or peer groups.

DAWN TO DUSK

In the sixth chapter of Deuteronomy, the great leader, Moses, addresses the nation of Israel at the end of his life. He knows his time with the people is coming to an end, and brings them all together to give them one final address. When I consider that occasion I imagine that choosing your final words would be quite a significant and daunting task. I imagine he would want to leave the people with the most important ordinances he could articulate. This was going to be the last message they would ever hear from him. What did he leave them with? In his last ever address, Moses chose to give the nation of Israel a pattern for parenting. Remarkable!

> *You shall love the LORD your God with all your heart, with all your soul, and with all your strength. And these words which I command you today shall be in your heart. You shall teach them diligently to your children, and shall talk of them when you sit in your house, when you walk by the way, when you lie down, and when you rise up.*
>
> *Deuteronomy 6:5-7 (NKJV)*

Verse 7 lays out four poignant times of the day in which families can seize God-ordained moments to enrich the lives of our loved ones – when you sit in your house, when you walk by the way, when you lie down, and when you rise up.

Four times a day, in different roles and modes and forums, Moses encouraged God's people, Israel, to set deep foundations in the hearts of each coming generation. Thousands of years may have passed since Moses' address to the Israelites in Deuteronomy chapter 6, but the principles have not changed; and the effectiveness of this model is infallible. Daily, weekly, and yearly rhythms are essential for the health of an individual. And every parent must be mindful, and intentional, to seize these rhythms in a proactive and constructive fashion.

Hungry Hearts

When You Sit In Your House

One of my greatest passions is the family table. As I've ministered over the years on this particular topic, I am both exceedingly blessed, and surprised, at the power it holds to strike a nerve in the hearts of those hearing. I am on a mission to restore the family table. To bring it back as the centrepiece of the home and the family.

I've come to learn how rare it is, these days, for a family to sit around a table together regularly, with crockery and cutlery, and a home-made meal. And to do this in a casual relaxed and unrushed setting. Truly rare indeed. I have come to realise that many homes don't even have a dining table any more.

Today's meal times are isolated and independent experiences, in front of a TV, or a computer, on a couch, or in a bedroom, where every family member might even fend for themselves, eating different instant meals separately. And when I paint a picture of what it could, and should, look like in the home, the response I have is overwhelming. I often receive messages from people who tell me that they have gone out to buy a dining table in response to this message. I receive photos of families proudly sitting around a table for the first time. Beaming faces leaning over table settings and food together.

It is a personal fascination of mine. I've learned that there are direct correlations between communal meal time experiences, and a child's future adult flourishing. Research over decades, and in different cultures, tells a compelling story. Children in homes where the family table is central, are less prone to destructive behaviours, such as drug abuse, promiscuity, and crime. These children have decreased rates of anxiety and depression. They have increased propensities towards stable careers, wealth, marriage, and physical health. Children who are taught how to use a knife and fork, and politely conduct themselves in a conversation around a meal, do exponentially better in their future lives than their friends who are never given these opportunities.

The tables we offer them at home literally determine the tables they may, or may not, sit at as adults. The children of the godly could be, and should be, sitting at tables of influence as adults, bringing the culture of Heaven into all the spheres of society. My role as a parent is to instil Biblical morality in the heart of my child, and to teach them how to hold a knife and fork. To offer them a seat at the table of life.

Repeated studies have further found that the children, who grew up in homes where a family table is absent, are regularly found in the homes of their friends where a family table is present.

In our home, it's dinner every night at 5:30pm. There are nine of us, and rapidly the older ones are building lives with careers and licenses, professional pursuits, and social engagements. The general rule at home is that everyone is assumed to be attending dinner unless they've communicated otherwise. Every night the table is set, the meal is served, and together we recount the moments of our individual days. Jared and I gently, and intentionally, guide the conversation. We come back to our family values throughout those conversations every night. We celebrate where values have been embodied. We draw lessons from the moments, where values have been compromised. We each make observations from the day, and troubleshoot with each other. It's a beautiful time of culture setting, and group accountability. It's a type of group-think, that strengthens and emboldens everyone present.

It is at the table that young children learn how to converse. They have to be taught through observation and correction. They watch the flow of information move around a table. They learn how to interact. They learn when it is appropriate to speak, and when it is appropriate to listen. They learn how to celebrate other people's ideas and, occasionally, assert their own. This is a skill that is being lost in our society.

Often parents despair at the behaviour of their children in public settings. What is established at the family table has consequences for every other area of a child's life. There is considerable coaching, and consistent dialogue, that must go into teaching a child how to hold themselves in public. A child needs to understand that, being in a public setting, is a privilege, and that they must respect others. We are teaching them emotional intelligence through self-awareness and social awareness. Coaching beforehand, and celebrating when they meet expectations, is the relentless responsibility of a parent who wants their child to thrive.

The truth is, when a child is disruptive in public, it reflects on the guidance they are receiving at home. We cannot simply blame personalities, or the long list of conditions that are commonly discussed today. If a parent is not doing their part in coaching, that child has no clear boundaries to help structure their life. Children can be taught the consequences, and rewards, of healthy social engagement, and this foundation is built within the home.

We slow a child down, and calmly talk them through the evening process. We gently coach them on what the goals are, and what it is we're aiming for. We treat them as dignified beings who have a valued presence. We build them up to be confident, engaging people, who can make eye contact, and hold intelligent conversation. It is the breath of Heaven, put back into a delicate young soul charged in our care; the child that Heaven has entrusted us to steward. These ones are filled with the destiny of Heaven, the potential of the divine, and it is our privilege and responsibility to build and draw that out into a world that so desperately needs peace, order and breakthrough.

At meal times, together around the table, we put our devices out of reach, and out of sight. We decline all distractions to be present to one another, in a sacred space of community and communion. The family table could be the most powerful formative altar of your life, and the lives of your family.

Backseat Bandits

When You Walk By The Way

I remember the day my oldest child got her license, and drove away for the first time. I suddenly realised I would very rarely have that captive moment with her again, where we would travel together in the car on the way to an appointment, or social engagement. Suddenly, with the keys to her own vehicle, a season had ended for a rich opportunity of input.

It is the 'lasts' that catch us off guard sometimes. Like the time I dismantled my youngest child's crib once he had outgrown it. I thought nothing of it at the time until I walked back into the room later that day, and the crib was no longer there. Sorrow struck my heart as I realised I had missed a moment to recognise, and savour, the end of an era. It was the same awe-inspiring reckoning that filled my heart when my oldest daughter drove away that day. I realized the travel time together had come to an abrupt end.

Not only that, being another designated driver in the family meant that she could taxi around other children, further reducing our time as parents with them in the car. And so not only had my time in the car with her come to an end, but also my time in the car with the other children would somewhat decrease as well with her being able to drive them from place to place. I say all this because we must realise the potency of the moment we have with our children in car rides between places.

As they grew, we encouraged our children not to spend drive time on their devices, or with earphones in, blocking out the conversations happening in the car. Just the other day, on the school drive-through, I noticed a young girl, probably about 15, in the passenger seat with, who I assumed, was her father. They seemed completely disconnected, sitting just centimetres apart. She had her earphones in, and was gazing out the window. I felt a deep sadness thinking about how easy it is, for even the closest relationships, to drift into distance and indifference.

I found myself reflecting on what this might mean for her engagement with the world beyond that car. How has she been shown to treat others? How is she learning to be attentive, kind, and generous to the people around her?

We certainly have our work cut out for us, as Moses so aptly pointed out. These are the moments we must seize to instil the right values in our children, not only for their own growth, but also for the sake of the wider culture and society.

Our modern day *'walking by the way'* is that precious social, and relational setting, in the car between places. When we seize these moments, we encourage our families to recognise how to honour a person's presence, and place value on those who are in immediate proximity with us. We are not teaching our children to wait for others to engage with, dote on, and compliment them first. We teach our children how to look outside of themselves as contributors, rather than self-oriented consumers. We teach our children how to build up, and celebrate, those around us through our positive and intentional interaction with them.

Moses instructed the people to talk about the ways of God as they 'walked by the way'. In these spaces we are side-by-side with our child. In these moments, rich learning and connection can be made. Parents should turn down the radio, and limit outside interruptions via phone calls, in order to be able to open dialogue with the young ones in the car. There are two very distinct opportunities in these drivetime moments – one being on the way to an event, and the other being on the drive after the event. Each scenario presents a unique set of opportunities.

Arrivals: Coaching

This is such a potent opportunity for coaching, the drive to any event. It's a time to remind ourselves of who we are, and how we present ourselves to the world. It is a time to build them up. It's a time to give them confidence. It's a time to pre-empt the scenarios that they may encounter in the coming hours. This is when I draw on mental notes I've made from previous social encounters, where I can coach the children around desired behaviour in an encouraging and empowering way. Setting them up with confidence to win.

One of the greatest tools for emotional intelligence is mental preparation. Travel time to an event is this opportunity. We teach the kids what to expect, and how to respond. We discuss the various potential scenarios, and we brainstorm appropriate behaviour in alignment with family values. And we always bring desired outcomes back to servant-hearted leadership, mission, purpose, and calling. We're never setting our children up to be self-preserving in their behaviour, but we are always teaching our children to be generous servant-hearted leaders in every single setting they face. We remind them that the call of Heaven is on their lives, and that they are destined to make a Kingdom impact in the spaces that the Lord has positioned them. These little backseat bandits are poised, and ready, with a mission from Heaven.

Departures: Celebration

Imagine you arrive at the destination and, during the course of the social engagement, you witness behaviour in your child that was less than desirable. It's not hard to imagine for most of us.

Firstly, we should be careful that we do not publicly humiliate our children with a jarring correction there in the moment, in front of an audience. We gently pull them aside and quietly encourage them to remember what we agreed on in the car. We clarify who we are, but we tuck that moment away in our memory for a future coaching opportunity, and we resist the urge to unleash negative feedback in the car ride home. I have found that coaching up front is always more powerful than critical feedback afterwards. So I make a mental note, and remember to use that experience as the forward coaching moment in the next drive to a social engagement.

We use the departure travel times for conversations around experiences, and encounters, from that day or from a particular social setting. When the children were young, we would use terms like highs and lows, and pits and peaks. Each member of the car ride would summarise that day, and their experiences in those ways. This provides an insight into each other's world, and opens up value-driven discussion every time. It's usually light-hearted and casual, but enough to offer group learning, and troubleshooting, for a team type environment in close proximity.

Sleepy Ears

When You Lie Down

I could write an entire book on this one moment in a child's day. I have seen how powerful and potent these sleepy moments are. And I could tell volumes of personal stories, where breakthroughs have taken place in the strategies I've applied in these quiet moments at the end of the day. If there's one thing you take away from the next few paragraphs, it's this: do not give away or undervalue the bedtime routine.

I am a strategic thinker. I'm always looking for patterns. I don't want to spend redundant time re-creating the wheel if I can learn from other people, from history, and from events. I'm a people-watcher, and an incessant question-asker. In the decade I spent leading youth ministry, I saw thousands of teenagers interact with the world. I developed a growing suspicion that a child's flourishing was not just dependent on personality and intellect, because I saw the full spectrum of personalities play out in different ways. I became increasingly aware that, who a young person would become, was dependent on far more than genetics and predispositions. I started to make time with the parents whose young people were buoyant, and wise among their peers. I was looking for patterns and clues. We all know there's no manual for parents, but I was convinced there must have been common factors that effectively build, and prepare, a young person for the fierce world.

There was one common theme which emerged. I was surprised to hear parent after parent tell me that they still sat on the end of their teenager's bed every single night. These teenagers, both male and female, had parents who prioritised the final moments of every day with them. I was blown away and, although this was a practice I had already been doing with my own very small children, I took on a more sincere approach to it.

Having both male and female children, I've learned the unique needs they each have in that most intimate moment of their day. Boys, in particular, withhold sharing much all day. They are far less expressive and verbal than their sisters. I found that my sons waited for their time with me at bedtime to be able to privately disclose the most sensitive parts of their day. My sons would come and find me, to tuck them into bed right into the teen years. They would pursue me for that time even more than the girls, and quietly ask me questions they didn't want to be heard in the earshot of others. As they grew, I felt more and more privileged to be invited into those spaces of their hearts. They learned I could be the first and safest, most trustworthy place to brainstorm hard things with.

I had encouraged them repetitively, over the years, that no topic was ever off-limits, and they took me up on that as I offered them those moments every day in the quiet dim lights. I was undone by the sacred privilege they would trust me with. My heart ached when I realised how many men have grown up without ever having this opportunity. Grown men, walking into the world, not knowing how to debrief intimate details. I suppose it is the great majority of our male population who have not had this opportunity in their formative years – questions unanswered, griefs not processed, insecurities and doubts never put to ease. They may never have learned how to be vulnerable, or how to form an intimate connection. Oh what dire prospects! Our sons need our time.

In a different way, my daughters drew their sense of self-worth from those moments in the dark. Our conversation was personal and vulnerable. They would share their social pains with me, and often they would weep. We would turn the tears into prayers, and believe together for the hand of God to provide answers and solutions. Sometimes those prayers would continue every night for months, and even years, but the breakthrough always came and, perhaps, more powerful than the breakthrough itself was the fact that these delicate beings, in their formative years, knew that they had a safe place at the end of every single day.

For both the sons and the daughters, we must resist the urge to be a lecturer or a disciplinarian. In these intimate moments we are a listening ear of compassion and safety, we are mild towards them. "It's hard work being a teenager," is something I often found myself saying to them. I validated the treacherous social terrain they would navigate each day, and bond our hearts together as we would turn our struggles towards the face of God. These were truly divine moments.

When they are younger, their little sleepy ears are like access points to the soul and spirit. As they drift off into that slumber space, they are more receptive than any other time in the day to receive the words that we say. So we choose our words delicately, and intentionally, in those moments. I found that with my more robust children, if I waited till they were in the in-between space of wake and slumber, still conscious enough to hear my words, and yet sleepy enough to be still, I would speak the destiny of Heaven into those ears. Little moans of agreement would rumble in their chests, and I revelled in the thought that I could send them off to sleep with the echo of the Father's song singing over them.

One of my daughters is particularly a little bit cheekier than the others. It was not unusual for her to present a counter argument to just about anything that was ever said, all with a cheeky smirk and a sparkly sideways glance. She had a constant urge to challenge the status quo. When she was about three years of age she developed a new habit at bedtime. She started rejecting the positive confessions I made over her as I always had done at the bedtime routine.

"You are so beautiful," I would say to her.

"No, I'm not," she would respond.

"Yes, you are made so beautifully by the hand of God. You're clever and kind and special."

"No, I'm not."

Night after night, I was distraught that she would reject life-giving truths, and I became concerned with the impact that could be having in her heart. I remember one night walking out of her room feeling defeated. I sat in the play room, on a miniature chair, with my head in my hands. I prayed.

"Lord, how will I get these confessions into her heart if she keeps turning them away?"

"Wait until she's almost asleep and say it then," was the response I felt in my spirit.

The next night that's exactly what I did. We did our usual Bible time and prayer routine, and I just laid on the bed with her until she got sleepy. At that point I started to tell her how beautiful and kind she was.

"Mmmhmmmm," a murmuring hum of agreement vibrated in her belly. She had received the confession of Heaven.

This same daughter was also the child who would call out numerous times, with numerous requests, each night, and occasionally she ventured out to find us. While her sister, the rule keeper, lay silently in her bed after the tuck-in moment, this particular little one always had one hundred things to do when the lights were turned down. I know I'm not telling an unusual story. If we had a camera in any young family's home this would be a most common scene, much to the despair of parents all over the world. Knowing that I didn't want her last moments to be stern disciplinary moments, I asked the Lord for a strategy.

A comfortable high wing-back armchair became my daily devotional space for a season. After reading with them, praying with them, and turning down the lights just enough to dim the space without losing visibility, I would sit in this armchair, night after night, for almost two years. I sat with the Scriptures, my journal and a pen, and she would quietly watch me. She knew she wasn't allowed to interrupt me, but she would watch. Waves of peace, washing over her in the comfort of my presence, changed her bedtime experience. And for me those journals became preaching content many decades later. Of course, at the time I had no premonition the Lord would be resourcing me with revelation to shepherd a future flock of His.

My point is this. Be present to your seasons, and know that family ministry is the first ministry. The Lord is not surprised by your circumstance, or season. He is also outside of time, and the author and finisher of your faith. They say the days are long but the years are short. Invest the days well, because the years will escape you swiftly. What remains are the investments and the values laid as foundations.

New Beginnings

When You Rise

Mornings can be mayhem! But they really shouldn't be. One of the surprising benefits of prioritising these four rhythms every day is that they create a predictability for each member of our families to enjoy. We will talk more about rhythms in the next section, and one of the ways that rhythms benefit our day is in the success of the morning routine.

Most children are early risers, which may be the first obstacle you need to overcome. They are wise enough, and receptive enough, to understand the boundaries around what time to get up in the morning. Our second youngest daughter was notorious for waking up early, and waking her younger roommate-sister before the Sun. We bought her a fun digital bedside clock, and taught her numbers. She was very clearly instructed that she would not be allowed to leave her room, or make a sound, until there was a six at the front of the number. I'm constantly amazed with how responsive children are when they're entrusted with responsibility, and so she was. We didn't hear from her again before 6am.

We also had laminated charts for each of our children, when they were young, and still learning about the new beginnings of each day. This included the order of priority, and things they needed to achieve without assistance. The charts are pictorial checkbox lists, laminated for checking off with whiteboard markers, to be cleaned off each day. They had to make their bed before leaving a bedroom, arrange breakfast for themselves, or with the assistance of a sibling or parent. They had to feed the pets before sitting down to eat for themselves.

The breakfast table itself, while chaotic at times, is a beautiful communal space, where conversations and plans for the day are shared. Usually fresh minds are quite humorous and generous. Their charts reminded them to clean their own breakfast dishes, and the breakfast bench, and move on to teeth, wardrobe, hair, and preparing backpacks with supplies for the day. If they ever asked what was needed to be done, they would be directed back to the laminated check chart, and they would get themselves back on track.

After a little while of consistent effort, the buzz of self-leadership and personal responsibility is palatable when it's done well. Parents move through the house as positive coaches, sharing encouraging words, and celebrating the industrious display. It's the time of the day where teamwork is most in the atmosphere. Everyone recognises the part they play to get the day rolling, and to have everyone where they need to be at the right time. This is important parenting, to teach your child to take responsibility for themselves, and to be part of the team at the beginning of the day.

If you feel that your schedule, or vocation, prevents you from being present with your family in the mornings and evenings, I would gently yet firmly encourage you to consider whether a change is needed. The cost of absence is high. We cannot truly claim to be 'providing' for a family if we are never present with them.

The Lord has trusted the next generation into our care. There is no income, no career, no neon sign, or accolade, that is worth the loss of the next generation. I am convinced we can do both, and we can do them both exceptionally well. Our priority must be sowing the ordinances of Scripture into our families, before any other thing draws us away. We must ensure that the foundations of the Kingdom are laid in our families. When we sit in our homes, walk by way, lie in our beds, and rise in the morning. These four foundational moments of every day must be the priority of our lives. Everything else flows after this has been established.

SECTION THREE

Feast & Fire

THOU SHALT PARTY

My childhood was a humble one. I was the eldest of three daughters, to an immigrant family. My mother and father fled communist Poland in the 1980s. When the plane landed in Brisbane, Australia, with my parents on board, my mother was heavily pregnant with me, and I was born only weeks later, while they were staying in a short-term processing facility in Wacol, Brisbane.

This facility was an arrangement of small demountable buildings, situated beside one another, where others like my parents would live communally while they awaited their approvals to be processed before starting a new life. This camp was a place where my parents made their first acquaintances with all of the native Australian wildlife. Insects, snakes, loud obnoxious birds, spiders, and the milder, cuddlier mammals that call Australia home.

I was Australian by birth, and very much Polish by blood and culture. My first language was Polish, and I went to my first day of primary school not speaking a word of English.

We didn't have a lot while I was growing up. Homes were humble, furniture was sparse, and there was rarely enough finance for indulgence or decadence.

I still treasure the sepia tone photographs of myself, in the highchair of a bare dining room, with my parents on either side. The warm tones of images that depict joy and contentment in the face of a child who was living in a home where creative celebration was a family value, and a cultural norm.

Embedded in the DNA of European nations is a value for hospitality and generosity. This value transcends materialistic means. You don't need a lot of money to eat well, celebrate well, and enjoy the true riches of life. I watched my parents, and grandparents, over deep pots on the stove for days on end, in the lead up to significant celebrations and events. I heard them plan for days, weeks, and months in advance. Celebration was important. Food was important. Being together was important. Wealth was not a currency in a bank account. It was a state of the heart.

Although they had very little, my parents never missed a birthday, a Christmas, or an Easter celebration. Cakes and gifts were decorated, and wrapped with deep intentionality and bright extravagant detail. As a child, I always felt valued and loved. I always felt seen and important. I knew to the core of my being that I had been thought of. I knew because of the way they lived their priorities.

Much of what we had was home-made, including some of our clothes. The attention to detail, and intricate beauty, sewn into every work, communicated resounding messages of value. We didn't have a lot, but we had everything.

I thought it was very normal until, of course, I started experiencing the way other families lived. But culture shock was not the only rude awakening I was on course for.

It was the Christmas after my 11th birthday that my life came to a grinding halt. Looking out towards the front portico, I could see the Christmas tree in my peripheral on the left. The decorations were bright and patterned, with coloured stringed lights that had frosted casings. The tree was not the focus of my view on that day. Looking straight ahead I could see packed suitcases on the front doorstep. Dad was leaving. He had worked a job that regularly took him away for weeks at a time. We would miss him while he was away, and savour the short stints of time when he returned home. This particular day was different from the other times his bags were packed. This time he was leaving for good.

My parents had both worked hard. My mother worked shifts at the hospital, and father did fly-in-fly-out work. Things between them deteriorated over the years. Since it is their story to tell, not mine, I'll leave it there. Only to say I knew, all of a sudden that morning, looking through the front door at that suitcase, that life would never ever be the same again.

The little my parents had built up over the years, was divided in settlement hearings over finance and property, and we were thrown back into days of lack. My mother picked up as much work as she could to support her three daughters. We moved into a tiny home and, even in its meagreness, it was nothing short of miraculous provision from the Hand of the God, who she only just come to encounter through her recent Salvation experience.

Coming into my teen years, I was becoming a lot more aware of her efforts and her sacrifice. Growing older now, my sisters and I had responsibilities around the house, and in the family. In all the hardship, Mum still never missed a birthday, a Christmas, or an Easter celebration. Cakes and gifts were still as intentional and beautiful as ever. She continued to prioritise family holidays on a budget, where she would often go without in order to create moments of celebration for our little family. She prayed a lot these days.

My two sisters and I joined her in the Church she was attending. We found Salvation, restoration, meaning and destiny. Though I strayed over the teen years, I never doubted the existence and the kindness of God. By the time I was a young adult, and had started seeing the fruit of poor decisions in my life, I knew where to turn.

A university friend invited me to attend a service in his Church community. That night was a turning point, and the start of my life. I began regularly attending that Church. I met Sam there, we got engaged, we got married and, soon to my surprise, stepped into the ministry of leading the teenagers.

Sam didn't always see the necessity for my extravagance when it came to dinner parties, birthdays, and holidays. He was surprised that I could find any excuse to celebrate. On the first day of the school term, I would insist that we took the kids out for milkshakes. On the last day of the school term, I would insist that we took the kids out for milkshakes. If there was a first-place ribbon in a sporting event there was another reason to celebrate. A good report card meant an ice-cream date. Gifts were non-negotiable. Birthday parties every year. Family holidays included meal plans, and a feast every single night. He was surprised at the lengths I would go to when hosting a dinner, or a party, at our home. One time I made a birthday cake for my daughter that took six days to prepare. It was a castle with towers and vines, the size of a small table. Over the years he came to appreciate the celebrations, and the holidays, and eventually became even more particular than me.

In a deep study of the Spiritual Disciplines, my curiosity was triggered when I noticed Celebration on the list of Spiritual Disciplines. As I began to study Celebration for the next fortnight, I was brought to my knees, brought to tears, and set alight. God loves to party!

In His kindness, the Lord instituted feasts, festivals, and periods of rest, into the rhythms of community and personal life. These intentional times, and their regularity, had significant spiritual implications. The ordinances God gave us around celebration were to keep us excited and positive, to help us add value to our experience in life, to enjoy each other, to appreciate successes, and to stay connected with Him. God knew that, without intentional moments of celebration, pause, and reflection, His beloved ones would grow weary. Without these times of grateful remembrance, our human nature tends to get lost in the grind of culture and daily life. What was meant for our thriving and prosperity, can easily be reduced to mere survival.

In His wisdom and kindness, God understood that our frail human condition could not endure all that life would bring, without regular moments of joy and meaningful connection. I can testify to the knowing in His heart – that life on this fallen planet would take its toll. He knew we would face trials, suffer loss, and experience moments that would deplete our souls. He knew that, to fully embrace the days He would give us, our humanity would need space to breathe.

He also knew that our children would lose their sense of identity without a meaningful connection through family and community celebration. In His wisdom, He recognised the urgent need. A child connected to the family narrative would grow with deep foundations, and confidence to face an outside world. Without it that same child would question their own intrinsic value, and vulnerably search that same fallen world for answers – a world that was rigged against them – without an internal compass for orientation.

So, in the Old Testament, God commanded His people to celebrate and rest. He gave them guidelines on how, when and why. Many of the observances He gave were punishable if not observed, sometimes punishable even by death. I wonder, if He had written a separate code of conduct similar to the Ten Commandments, but related instead to the Spiritual disciplines, whether the discipline of celebration would be called 'Thou Shalt Party'.

The Lord was serious when He mandated the feasts, festivals, and rests. It is as though He was saying to us, "Thou Shalt Party. Or else! Or else you'll break."

> *We cannot break the Ten Commandments. We can only break ourselves against them — or else, by keeping them, rise through them to the fullness of freedom under God. God means us to be free. With divine daring, He gave us the power of choice.*
>
> *Cecil B. DeMille*

Nothing could be truer, especially in the case of the Spiritual nature of celebration and rest – without them we break ourselves.

It amazes me how many people neglect to celebrate milestones, and special moments, with those they love most. In our consumer-driven culture, with its constant pursuit of material gain, we often rush from week to week, month to month, year to year, rarely pausing to acknowledge or enjoy our own successes, or those of the people around us. In doing so, we trade a life of meaning for a life of mere survival, or worse, mere existence. This is not the life the Lord intends for those He loves.

I realised that the slow societal erosion of these values has degenerated the core of the human form. We have lost the art of celebration. We have ceased to understand what true rest really is. We have lost the deep richness of dynamic family rhythms. As a result, we are merely shadows of who He originally intended us to be, with each passing generation breaking down further and further. As I sat under the weight and the gravity of the revelation being opened to me as I studied, I was truly moved that the Lord was making provisions for me, and for my family, and for all his people, to find meaning and enjoyment in the days He has set before us. He was showing us how to lay deep unshakeable foundations, how to find meaning, and how to secure strength into the future.

HIDDEN IN PLAIN SIGHT

Everything in Scripture points to Jesus.

From the beginning of time, in the garden of Eden, there are layers and echoes and foreshadowings of Christ, all pointing to His life, death, resurrection, and the provision of the Holy Spirit. The Old Testament points forward to Jesus. The New Testament reflects back on His life. He is not just the centre, He is everything. The Godhead – Father, Son, Holy Spirit – speaks of Jesus. All of Scripture, all of history, all of humanity.

Sometimes this seems obvious, other times the revealing of new truths has the power to shake us, and reform us. Many times I have been utterly struck as I have committed to deeper study. The layers of revelation are infinite and unending. The specific learning about feasts, festivals, and rests ordained by the Lord, have revolutionised my life, and my perspective of Yahweh, Elohim, the Lord – Jesus. He is a genius, kind and provisional. To walk in the ways He has ordained leads to great reward, and preserves us from our own faults, foolishness, and presumptuousness. To walk in His ways is to strengthen and fortify ourselves.

> The law of the Lord is ***perfect,***
> ***reviving the soul;***
> the testimony of the Lord is ***sure,***
> making ***wise the simple;***
> the precepts of the Lord are ***right,***
> ***rejoicing the heart;***

the commandment of the Lord is ***pure***,
enlightening the eyes;
the fear of the Lord is ***clean***,
enduring forever;
the rules of the Lord are true,
and righteous altogether.
More to be desired are they than gold,
even much fine gold;
sweeter also than honey
and drippings of the honeycomb.
Moreover, ***by them is your servant warned***;
in keeping them there is great reward.
Who can discern his errors?
Declare me innocent from ***hidden faults***.
Keep back your servant also from ***presumptuous sins***;
let them not have dominion over me!
Then I shall be blameless,
and innocent of great transgression.
Psalm 19:7-13 (ESV)

Some 4,000 years passed between Adam and Jesus and, in the narrative of Scripture, we see 130 generations across the face of the Earth interacting with the Lord, and each other, in that time. The Lord ever-present, revealing Himself, and pointing to the Son. Jesus was woven into the heart of the feasts, festivals, and Sabbath rests. Thousands of years before His physical arrival as a man, the Lord had invited us to gather around His divine Son, as families and communities.

The seven key feasts and celebrations of the Old Testament are breathtaking foreshadowings of Jesus. The Feast of Passover, Unleavened Bread, First Fruits, and Pentecost, were all fulfilled in Jesus' life, death and resurrection, and ascension. There He was all along, hidden in plain sight, as a force present to all humanity. It was this revelation that brought me low that day. The Lord, and His infinite all knowingness, making provisions for His most unaware and beloved ones.

"Not only will you rest and celebrate for the wealth of your own souls," I heard the Lord whisper over us, as I learned of how He handed down His ordinances. "But in doing so, your spirits will recognise the Messiah and Saviour you so long for and, one day, you will behold Him altogether. He will forever be the centre of these identity-forming moments, initially in anticipation, and finally in realised completion. My Son will ever be your source of meaning and regeneration."

BIBLICAL FEASTS / CELEBRATIONS					
	CELEBRATE / COMMEMORATE	*TRADITION*	*THEME*	*SIGNIFIES*	*FULFILLED*
PASSOVER (Exodus 12 and Leviticus 23)	Lamb Blood on door posts – sparing first-born	Passover meal	Forgiveness	Christ as the perfect sacrifice	Crucifixion
UNLEAVENED BREAD (Exodus 12 & 13 and Leviticus 23)	Exodus from Egypt – no time for bread to rise (leaven)	Clean house – remove leaven	Purity / Sanctification	Humanity's complete separation from the world	Burial
FIRST FRUITS (Leviticus 23)	First part of the barley harvest	Bring a first fruits offering	Resurrection	Jesus as the 'first-fruit' offering	Resurrection
PENTECOST (Leviticus 23)	End of barley, beginning of wheat harvest	2 Loaves: 1 Leavened (Gentile); 1 Unleavened (Jew)	Jew & Gentile	Birth of the Church	Holy Spirit 3,000 added (Both Jew & Gentile)
TRUMPETS (Leviticus 23)	Ushering in the Sabbatical Month	Stop work to worship at Trumpet Sound	Christ's return	Christ's second coming Judgement of the world	FUTURE
ATONEMENT (Leviticus 16 and 23)	Our inability to make ourselves right with God	Fasting Priests make sacrifices for the people	Righteousness	Removal of people's sin	FUTURE
TABERNACLES (Leviticus 23)	God's provision in the wilderness	Sacrifices Booths made of palm branches	Kingdom	Christ dwelling and reigning with mankind again	FUTURE

OTHER OBSERVANCES					
Sabbath Day Weekly (Punishable) (Genesis 2 and Exodus 20)	God rested on seventh day	No labour (Family, servants, strangers, even animals)	Rest To cease or abstain		
Sabbath Year Seventh year (Exodus 23 and Leviticus 25)	God rested on seventh day	Resting land for a year to replenish and renew, Debts pardoned	Rest To cease or abstain		
Year of Jubilee (Every 49 years) (Leviticus 25)	All tribes living in Israel	Slaves released, Houses & Land reclaimed	Renewal		

The Feasts and Festivals were penned by Moses in chapter 23 of the book of Leviticus. Each of the seven celebrations and feasts commemorated an event. Each one had its own specific tradition and theme. Most remarkably, though, is what each of these feasts and celebrations signified in the life of our Lord, Jesus Christ. Though given by the Father thousands of years before the Son's appearance, they all pointed to Him; every single one, and we didn't even know it.

Not only do these celebrations give us pause to wonder in awe, and provide an anchor to our souls, but they actually memorialise the sacrifice and victory of the cross, and the empty tomb, the ascension, and the outpouring of the Holy Spirit. The evangelism and rebirth of humanity – every man, woman, and child – among every tribe and tongue in the Earth. What the Israelites could not have known in Egypt was that, through instituting these feasts, the Lord was foreshadowing the work of the coming Messiah. Every celebration was a prophetic act.

I remember the day I drew all the pieces together. I slipped down off the study chair, away from my computer, and sat as lowly as possible on the white tiled floor. When the Spirit of revelation settles on me, I often sense the tangible weight of it. I have to get down low.

This particular sunny afternoon was one of those rare and most precious moments. I wanted to simultaneously laugh and cry. What God ordained and mandated in the Old Testament, Christ would fulfil in His body, and in the Church that was to come. He cared for me in these ordinances of rest and celebration, but He was pointing to the Son, and to all of humanity. How wonderfully divine. As I spent time drawing together the Old Testament feasts being mirrored in the life of Christ and the early Church, the detail, consistency and significance rocked me to the core.

The Passover, being the one we are possibly the most familiar with, commemorated the lamb's blood on the doorposts of the Israelite's houses the night that the Lord would lead them out of Egypt. Every Hebrew family was instructed to slaughter a lamb that night, a spotless, perfect lamb, and smear its blood on the doorpost of their home. This very night the

Lord would carry out the final of the 10 plagues that were being played out in the nation of Egypt, in response to Pharaoh's hardened heart and refusal to release the people of God from captivity.

Already the water had turned into blood. Frogs, lice, flies, pestilence, boils, hail, locusts, and darkness had been poured out on this nation. The plagues came every time Pharaoh refused to let the people of Israel go. And, on this night, the final and most severe of the 10 plagues was about to take place. Every home in the nation would come under the power of the angel of death, and the first born of every family and livestock would die. Every family – except the Israelite families who had marked the doorposts of their homes with the blood of a spotless lamb. On this night the angel of death would recognise the doorpost marked with lamb's blood, and pass over those homes. The angel of death would only visit the homes which were not marked with the blood of the lamb.

This was the first ever *pass over*; and every year thereafter the Israelite community would remember this night. The annual Passover Festival signified forgiveness, covering, and protection. It also signified the substitutionary death of another to provide for our covering.

When Jesus sat with His disciples at the Last Supper, they were all together, celebrating the Passover meal that night. A room full of Hebrew men remembering the annual tradition of Passover from centuries past. Little did they recognise that this was the night where the perfect Lamb would give up His life.

As Jesus was breaking bread, and blessing the wine, their futile minds were not perceiving what was taking place before them. On this Passover night, in a private room shared by Jesus and His followers, the culmination of all those generations of Passover celebrations had come to its head. This Passover night would initiate the crucifixion of Christ – when the true Lamb of God would be sacrificed to pay the penalty of death for all humanity past, present, and future. What had been a remembrance of lamb's blood on doorposts of homes, was now going to be the Lamb's blood on the doorposts of our lives. What had been celebrated for centuries was being fulfilled in a once-and-for-all offering in the body of the perfect Lamb of God.

Immediately following the original Passover celebration, the Lord instituted the Feast of Unleavened Bread. This commemorated the urgent exodus from Egypt, when the people were instructed to take no yeast nor leaven with them as they hastened out of the nation of Egypt on foot. After losing his own son in the tenth plague, not only was Pharoah willing to release the Israelites, but he wanted them gone immediately. The people had no time for bread to rise. No time for leaven to take effect.

Keep in mind also that leaven has always been the picture of iniquity and sin. By leaving Egypt in such haste without leaven in the bread, they were symbolising a life without inequity, and without sin. A new destiny without the sin of the previous life being brought into it. Every year the Hebrew households would clean out the house, removing all leaven from the home. The theme, of course, was purity and sanctification, signifying humanity's complete separation from the world. Fast forward all those thousands of years, it was on this day that Jesus was buried. Burying sin all on behalf of all humanity – past, present, and future. Incredible.

Immediately following this celebration of Unleavened Bread, the people of Israel would have a Firstfruits celebration. Being an agricultural society, at this time they would bring the first part of the barley harvest as an offering to the temple of God. It was a beautiful, joyous occasion, when the offering of the beginning of harvest time was brought as worship. First fruits were the theme of their celebration. Bringing to the Lord the first of a greatly anticipated harvest. For hundreds of years, God's people would do this. Even at the time of Jesus, this was being celebrated in Jewish custom. It was on this exact day that Jesus rose from the dead, resurrected. Pause and consider this. Jesus resurrected as the first fruits offering on behalf of all mankind. The first resurrected Son. The first fruits of many more sons to come. One given as a first fruit offering, for the harvest of all sons and daughters.

And 50 days after Passover was the celebration of Pentecost, at the end of the barley season, and the beginning of the wheat harvest. At this beginning of the wheat harvest, Hebrew families would make two loaves of bread – one with leaven, and one without. What is remarkable is that the fulfilment of this celebration was at Pentecost, in the upper room, where the Holy Spirit fell with fire and tongues on the 120 people gathered and waiting.

From that outpouring, 3,000 people were added to the Church, and the Holy Spirit was given to both Jews and Gentiles. What the Hebrew people had been celebrating for the hundreds of years prior, by baking two loaves of different bread, was that was the day of the outpouring of the Holy Spirit. This foreshadowed the life of the Jew (unleavened bread), together with the life of the Gentile (leavened bread), being favoured by the Lord. The Church was born that day. The Spirit was poured out on all people without preference, pedigree, or distinction.

How extremely remarkable that, all those many years later, every single one of these feasts was fulfilled in perfect timing in the life, death, and resurrection of Jesus, and in the outpouring of the Holy Spirit in the early Church.

The awe and wonder of our beautiful Lord never cease to amaze me. The longer I spend in His Word, the more I learn of His nature, and the more blown away I become at His unending mystery and perfection. He has been intentional, and intricately involved, within our Salvation since the beginning of time. Christ is woven into every act of God. I am completely undone each time I see another layer of that mystery unfold before me, year after year, season after season. The Word of God continues to open up before us. An ocean of divine revelation constantly reveals the immeasurable depths of who He is.

And so here I was on my living room floor on an ordinary weekday afternoon, awed by what I discovered as I studied this Discipline of Celebration, in the ages-old Biblical commemorations and feasts.

As I dove deeper, I began to see that there was a pattern to God's plan for our daily, monthly, and annual lives. A perpetual cycle that included times of sacrifice, where we play the role of contributor, that would lead to times of celebration, where we enjoy the role of gratefulness. This then fed back into times of sacrifice, followed by celebration, followed by sacrifice. Around and around we would go, all in God's pattern for living. We see this pattern in the discipline of rest also. Six days of industrious activity, followed by one day of restful communion with the Lord in the form of Sabbath. We see the rhythms in all of the observances. We see our joining arms with Him in the rhythms of life.

> *Are you tired? Worn out? Burned out on religion? Come to me. Get away with me and you'll recover your life. I'll show you how to take a real rest.* ***Walk with me and work with me*** *– watch how I do it. Learn the* ***unforced rhythms of grace****. I won't lay anything heavy or ill-fitting on you. Keep company with me and you'll learn to live freely and lightly.*
> *Matthew 11:28-30 (MSG) .*

When we break this pattern, we begin to fill our lives with destructive types of striving and self-gratification. Our human tendencies wind up leading us into places of disorder. But, the patterns and plans of the Lord, lead us to live full, upbeat lives of great purpose, joy and, ultimately, fulfilment.

HEAVEN'S PARTY ETIQUETTE

She was turning 18. My first born. In every sense, my oldest daughter, Maja, is a remarkable human being. To celebrate her is an easy task. This birthday celebration was a little more difficult than I had hoped for on this occasion. We would be celebrating this milestone without her biological father. It was her first milestone without him since his passing. We had already celebrated Maja's high school graduation but, somehow, the 18th birthday weighed a little bit heavier. Her beautiful, adopted father and siblings, gathered with me as we set about making this event significant.

One of the things we will explore in a later chapter is the fact that the mandate for celebration doesn't change just because circumstances do. In fact, celebration gives meaning to every season, and a deeper meaning in the face of loss.

The Lord loves to party. We must all come to understand this if we are to know Him well. He really, really loves to party. He loves to make sure that everyone gets in on it. He outlines exactly how to give meaning to each of our celebrations. I call them His Party Rules, or Heaven's Party Etiquette. It's simple and potent all at the same time.

Interestingly, at the times the Lord gives these guidelines (in Deuteronomy and Nehemiah), His people were not always a flourishing light-hearted people. In Nehemiah's book, when the Lord reminds His people of the Party Etiquette, first given in Deuteronomy, they are broken people, living in the rubble of their tragic history of loss and struggle.

About 1,000 years after the law was given to the Israelites, following their exodus from Egypt, we find God's people in a devastating state. The nation of Israel has divided into two kingdoms: Israel in the north and Judah in the south. Both kingdoms were conquered, their people sent into exile and captivity. All the iconic national landmarks lay waste, destroyed by enemies, and God's people were a far cry from who they once were as a unified nation under David and Solomon.

After Judah's exiles return from Babylon to their homeland, two leaders rise up out of the remnant – Nehemiah the governor, and Ezra the priest. Their two books in Scripture run simultaneously. Both feature the rebuilding efforts of the city and, while they work together to rebuild the broken walls of God's city, they must rebuild the heart of the people as well. Nehemiah famously reads the Book of the Law of God in the hearing of all the people. They hear a stunning recount of God's original intention towards His people, who should be free and prosperous. The heart of the Israelite community aches under the hearing of these words.

> *So they read from the Book of the Law of God distinctly, faithfully amplifying and giving the sense so that [the people] understood the reading. And Nehemiah, who was the governor, and Ezra the priest and scribe, and the Levites who taught the people said to all of them, "This day is holy to the Lord your God; mourn not nor weep." For all the people wept when they heard the words of the Law. Then [Ezra] told them, "Go your way,* ***eat the fat, drink the sweet drink****, and send portions to him for whom nothing is prepared; for this day is holy to our Lord. And be not grieved and depressed, for the joy of the Lord is your strength and stronghold." So the Levites quieted all the people, saying, "Be still, for the day is holy. And do not be grieved and sad." And all the people went their way to eat, drink, send portions, and* ***make great rejoicing****, for they had understood the words that were declared to them.*
>
> *Nehemiah 8:8-12 (AMPC)*

He is reading from the instructions that were given 1,000 years prior in the book of Deuteronomy. He is reading the passage of the Book of the Law that outlines exactly how to commemorate and celebrate, and feast, as a people in community with each other, and with their God.

> *And you shall rejoice before the Lord your God,* ***you and your son and daughter, your manservant and maidservant, and the Levite who is within your towns, the stranger or temporary resident, the fatherless, and the widow*** *who are among you, at the place in which the Lord your God chooses to make His Name [and His Presence] dwell. And you shall* ***[earnestly] remember*** *that you were a slave in Egypt, and you shall* ***be watchful and obey*** *these statutes. You shall observe the Feast of Tabernacles or Booths for seven days after you have gathered in from your threshing floor and wine vat. You shall* ***rejoice*** *in your feast,* ***you, your son and daughter, your manservant and maidservant, the Levite, the transient and the stranger, the fatherless, and the widow*** *who are within your towns.*
> *Deuteronomy 16:11-14 (AMPC)*

You may already have noticed it – God's outline for party etiquette; His party rules.

1. Echoes of Grace in our remembering
2. Joy's Harvest in our rejoicing
3. Tables of Abundance in our feasting
4. Hearts Rekindled in our recommitment
5. Homes of Haven in our inclusivity

Echoes Of Grace

One Sunday morning, the children and I were on our way to the church building early, all of us involved in our different areas of serving that day. This particular Sunday was the first anniversary of the passing of our husband and father, Sam.

I asked my daughter, Layla, how she was feeling.

"Good," she said. She continued, "I've been thinking, Mum, what if we woke up today with only the things we gave thanks for yesterday."

I was moved to the core. What a powerful and sobering thought.

When we gather together, to celebrate as families and communities, this is the time where we remember and give thanks for what the Lord has done. Stories are told, foundations are laid and strengthened, identity is built, and glory is given to God. We guard these moments, and we determine our confessions. Victory is found in the place of *right remembering*, and a confession that glorifies the truth of who God is. We sound the echoes of grace.

Just prior to this instruction given by Moses in the 16th chapter of Deuteronomy, we see Moses speak directly to families. As we have already seen, in his very last address to the people of Israel, Moses stresses the importance of family life, and family conversation. He talks to the matriarchs and the patriarchs about the importance, and the method, of passing on generational stories.

> *Write these commandments that I've given you today on your hearts.* ***Get them inside of you and then get them inside your children. Talk about them wherever you are,*** *sitting at home or walking in the street; talk about them from the time you get up in the morning to when you fall into bed at night. Tie them on your hands and foreheads as a reminder; inscribe them on the doorposts of your homes and on your city gates.*
>
> *Deuteronomy 6:7-9 (MSG)*

I find it remarkable that this was Moses' chosen topic of address, in his very last statement, to the people he led for decades through the most significant and extraordinary circumstances. Of all the things he could have taught that day, he chose to address families in their times of togetherness. Of all the altars he established and ordained in his time, and in his leadership, the pinnacle message at the end of his life was summarised and emphasised as the family altar, being the supreme altar of them all.

He knew that a nation's culture was built by the building block of the family, and the stories that would be passed down. The family table, and times of celebration, are the most sacred events. This is a place where stories are told. This is a place of remembrance. This is a place where we give context and meaning to experiences, memories, hopes, dreams, and to struggles. This is the place where parents can set foundations deep in the hearts of the next generation. The family table is a place for the shaping of identity.

As we all well know, this is the crisis of the generation we are in. Identity. Who am I? Whose am I? Where do I fit? What does it all mean? Where is my worth? And the worth of the things that the world is putting before me?

It is at the family table, and within family celebrations, where such yearning questions are answered. Satisfying those questions in the hearts of our children, and in the hearts of our family, is the greatest gift of confidence and mission we can give each of them. Moses knew what he was doing when he instructed parents to hold these times sacred. He knew what was at stake, and what could be lost in its absence.

In Moses' final address, was an echo of the Lord's intention for the ways in which to celebrate.

> *And you shall* ***earnestly remember*** *that you were a slave in Egypt, and you shall be watchful and obey these statutes.*
>
> *Deuteronomy 16:12 (ESV)*

The Lord reminded His people of the same thing in the days of Nehemiah, as He began to rebuild His people. The first Party Rule of God's celebration is *right remembrance* together in our families and communities. We must remember His good hand, and His mighty grace, in the threads of the tapestry of our own lives, and within history. This remembering, in the form of storytelling and testimony, is the first mandate for celebration. Making time to reflect and dream, making time to keep God's story as central will, in turn, impact perspective and reality.

Why is this important? We have all experienced the disparity of opinion between two people. Two football fans can have completely opposing perspectives about a course of play in a game. Two Church members can walk out of the same gathering with completely different experiences. How is it possible that one person can encounter the presence of God while another, in exactly the same gathering, can walk out with a critical spirit?

Because life is lived from perspective. Life is lived out of the mind and emotions, ultimately impacting the will. The Lord recognises that we must make time to remember the truth of His goodness, actively and regularly bringing it to our conscious recollection.

Our words carry power. Our words create worlds. At the beginning of time, the Lord used language not to communicate, but to create. Being made in His likeness, we too have the power of creation in our mouths. We lead our hearts by the confession of our words, and we create worlds for ourselves, our children, and our communities.

Our God, the Trinity, declared at creation He would make humanity in His own image. We have studied this Scripture at length already, but here we will find a new thread.

> *Then God said, "Let Us make man* ***in Our image,*** *according to Our likeness..." In the image of God He created him. Male and female He created them. Then God blessed them, and God said to them, "Be fruitful and multiply."*
> *Genesis 1:26-28 (NKJV)*

Much like many patterns in Scripture, we see trinities, and patterns of threes, woven throughout. The human frame, created in the pattern of the trinity, is a triune being. We are body, soul and spirit. The body is the temporal home we live in for the short life, but we are eternal also. Our spirits are being renewed in Christ, and our souls are actively engaged in our experiences. Of the three parts, it is the body and the soul that require the most leadership and discipleship.

Our souls also are triune, being made up of the mind, will, and emotions. The collection of writings in the Psalms are a stunning example of what it looks like to lead our own souls. The active and intentional engagement with the will, the thoughts, the emotions. How we think, how we perceive, and how we recall all, inform the narrative we tell ourselves. This narrative frames the life we create for ourselves, what we believe about ourselves, and what we believe about our God. What we recall and how we recall it is crucial.

Our first mandate in celebration is to create times of remembrance around the goodness of God, to tell of the echoes of grace we can see. We make these times of communal positive confession, through speeches, storytelling, and honour. We intentionally create spaces for reflection around the grace of God in our lives.

Joy's Harvest

Joy is etched into the heart of our God. It is the second fruit of the Spirit, preceded only by love (Galatians 5:22-23). Joy is a source of strength, and a motivator of Kingdom mission.

> *Looking unto Jesus, the author and finisher of our faith, who* ***for the joy that was set before Him endured the cross****, despising the shame, and has sat down at the right hand of the throne of God.*
>
> *Hebrews 12:2 (NKJV)*

As followers of Jesus, we have the most to celebrate. Because I was His joy at the point of His ultimate sacrifice, I have joy in my salvation. He turns our mourning into dancing. He places a crown on our heads instead of ashes. He sets tables before us in the midst of our adversaries and hardships. He is a man of sorrows who transforms sorrows. He is a liberator, and the clarion call to a new day. He is never at a loss, or without power. He is mighty and He is able. He is willing and He is generous. We can be the most joy-filled people in the Earth.

> *A merry heart does good, like medicine, But a broken spirit dries the bones.*
> *Proverbs 17:22 (NKJV)*

Unlike happiness, joy is not circumstantial, it is a state of being, and a fruit of the life-flow in our Spiritual beings. Joy is visible evidence of an invisible life-source. Circumstances are ever-changing, but our joy is secure, it is a constant reality. While pain is inevitable, it is misery that is optional because of who we are in Christ. We access joy in the Spirit, and dwell there. Joy is a truth, and a fruit, of our abiding lives in the vine. So when the Lord called His people to gather for celebration, He ordained laughter and rejoicing as a part of our celebration.

> *And **you shall rejoice** before the Lord your God*
> *Deuteronomy 16: 11-14 (AMPC)*

Our times together should be light-hearted, fun, and celebratory, where we give thanks for the past and we share in the hopes for the future. Ezra corrected the sombre mood among the people, as the Word was being read in their hearing. He specifically named it, and refuted it.

> *Then [Ezra] told them, Go your way, eat the fat, drink the sweet drink, and send portions to him for*

> *whom nothing is prepared; for this day is holy to our Lord.* ***And be not grieved and depressed, for the joy of the Lord is your strength and stronghold.***
>
> *So the Levites quieted all the people, saying, "Be still, for the day is holy. And do not be grieved and sad..." And all the people went their way to eat, drink, send portions, and make great rejoicing, for they had understood the words that were declared to them.*
>
> *Nehemiah 8:10-12 (AMPC)*

Among the people of God, when we celebrate, we deny the presence of heaviness, depression, or grief. Laugh! Have fun! Take up joy. Be strong in it! This passage is the origin of that famous Scripture we quote in part so often. The joy of the Lord is our strength. When we are not strong, He is! We celebrate His goodness in all seasons. These are the etiquette requirements of the Lord.

As with all of the enemy's work, the pure and life-giving origins of celebration have been usurped by the world as a perverted counterfeit. Celebration has been twisted, laced with substance abuse, and lewd destructive behaviours. Many find themselves down this wide road. What looks like a form of elation and escape and reprieve, is truly a path to bondage. Sadly, celebration has lost its beauty in the world. Our generation has lost its ability to celebrate in a healthy manner, as they have ventured further and further away from the heart of God.

And yet His people, remaining connected to Him, are ones who don't need placebos or artificial highs. In the purity of our hearts towards Him, we truly have a cause for rejoicing. We don't need empty substitutes. We have the real thing. We have life, and life in abundance. Our overflow is joy.

In a world that has lost its ability to celebrate in a healthy manner, our joyful celebration is a powerful witness. Unlike the world, our joy is genuine without a need for unnecessary trappings in order to lighten the spirits, or wash away our sorrows. Our celebration is a place where the joy of the

Lord is expressed, and love for one another is extended. This becomes the most powerful testimony to a world that is craving such authentic relief.

> *By this shall all [men] know that you are My disciples, if you love one another [if you keep on showing love among yourselves].*
> *John 13:35 (AMPC)*

As our family pulled together the plans for Maja's 18th birthday, her wish was for a dry celebration without a drop of alcohol. I am not insisting on any religious framework. There is a time, a place, and a proper way to enjoy wine with friends, and each person is guided by their own convictions in the Lord. But I celebrated Maja's choice to host a party that stood apart from her peers, many of who were also coming of age, still impressionable, and seeking life-giving examples. This same desire shaped our second daughter, Melody's, 18th birthday celebration the following year.

At both events, more than one hundred people gathered at our home. The speeches were moving, honouring, joy-filled, and inspiring. Friends, family, colleagues, and peers, surrounded our daughters in prayer. It was a remarkable sight, and times I will forever treasure. Every person present was touched. These are truly spiritual moments, ones that speak to the soul, and its deep longing for meaning.

These times are the harvest of joy. They remind me that, in the family of God, where we are surrounded by genuine life-giving people in deep communities over the long course. Communities who lift spirits with joy, who know, with extravagant intent, what it is to celebrate the goodness of God, and the community of His people. Our celebrations are places of genuine unadulterated laughter and encouragement, places of lifting one another up, and a realignment to joy.

In His grace and provision, the Lord knew that the source of our strength was the joy of our salvation in Him. He knew that, in creating intentional places and times of righteous celebration, we would be strengthened. Rejoicing is the posture of celebration in the Kingdom.

Tables Of Abundance

A number of years ago we received an invitation to celebrate a friend's birthday. Written on the invitation were the words BYO chairs, blankets, salads, drinks, and meat. I have found this type of invitation to be more and more common in our culture and, while I understand it, I find it hard to align it with the posture that Heaven shows us in Scripture. Hospitality is also written into the core of who I am, and I love that God values it too. We see it all the way through Scripture. Generosity and hospitality are the overflow of the Spirit's work in our lives. In fact, hospitality is one of the prerequisites for eldership in the New Testament.

In the Old Testament, we see incredible stories of generosity and hospitality. Abraham jumped and ran to prepare a banquet feast for three men who arrived unannounced at his tent. Hebrews recalls that exact moment by saying that he was 'entertaining angels without knowing it' (Hebrews 13:2). And Abraham certainly didn't know, until after the feast was given, at which point one of his guests revealed themselves to be the Lord. For Abraham, this moment became the culmination of all the previous promises the Lord had given him, and the final seal of approval on his life for an heir. What if he had asked His three guests to BYO?

A Hebrew household, in Biblical days, would always have a fattened calf in the field in preparation for celebration so that, if the need arose, they were ready at any given moment with extravagance to give thanks and celebrate. I love that kind of faith. Faith that is poised with anticipation. Faith that makes room for God. Faith that makes room for a miracle. Faith that makes room for others to join in. Faith that lives in a constant state of party.

Thanksgiving and celebration make room for God, and He inhabits that room in our lives. I wonder how many of us live our lives inviting God to visit, but asking Him to BYO and, while He's at it, we'd like Him to bring provisions for us too.

The third-party etiquette rule for celebrating God's way is to feast, and to feast well. To go all out and eat well at times of celebration. I can almost hear the Amens from here!

> *Then [Ezra] told them, Go your way,* ***eat the fat, drink the sweet drink, and send portions to him for whom nothing is prepared;*** *for this day is holy to our Lord. And be not grieved and depressed, for the joy of the Lord is your strength and stronghold.*
> *Nehemiah 8:10 (AMPC)*

Allow me to explain why this is a point that the Lord strained to make. In Biblical times, meat was rare and it was extravagant. What the Lord was actually telling his people was to go all out. He was encouraging them to shake off 'poverty thinking', 'slave mentality', and the 'lack' mindset that so easily creeps into our busy, pragmatic, resource-conscious lives. He was telling His people to be generous with their expense, and their preparation at special times of celebration. He was telling them to go above and beyond. The Lord was asking them to feast with their families, and to also provide for the poor, the sojourner, the alien. We are a people of hospitality, and a people of generosity. We mirror the nature and character of our God.

When we come together to celebrate in the presence of God, only the finest and most generous feast is fitting, for it is offered in honour of Him. While He does call us to fast, He also calls us to feast. Amazingly, the very first thing we're going to do in Heaven is feast and celebrate!

> *And the angel said to me, "Write this: Blessed are those who are invited to the marriage supper of the Lamb." And he said to me, "These are the true words of God."*
> *Revelation 19:9 (ESV)*

On one particularly busy day, many years ago, I ordered some delicious Thai food from a local restaurant for dinner. I transferred the meals from their plastic containers into serving bowls. I still displayed the table in a way that I felt honoured my family, and honoured that precious time we had together in the midst of a busy day.

The next day I prepared a meal myself. Nothing fancy, just simple, whole ingredients, spices and herbs, and the children milled around the house as I prepared it. As we gathered around the table, the family atmosphere was subtly different to the night before. The meal I had made was most certainly inferior to the cuisine the night before, and yet the atmosphere of the home, and at the dinner table, was more alive. The family were grateful and engaged. It was at that moment I realised that extravagance lies in the intentionality and the generosity of time, effort and thoughtfulness. A present-ness. I realised I wasn't only feeding their bodies; I was also feeding their souls.

There are definitely occasions when a greasy bucket from a fried chicken chain is exactly what the family craves and wants. Those moments are fun, those moments are real and raw. I have come to recognise the power of hospitality in the home. In a culture that wants everything to be microwaved and instant, where consumption is at an all-time high, there is a deeper yearning in our families and communities. The souls we're feeding feel validated, and valued, when extra effort is taken to be planned, present, and intentional for them. You don't have to be a seven-star chef, just someone who offers the simplicity of a rolled-up sleeve with a heart on it.

> *The heart of him who has understanding seeks knowledge, But the mouth of fools feeds on foolishness. All the days of the afflicted are evil,* ***But he who is of a merry heart has a continual feast.***
>
> *Proverbs 15:14–15 (NKJV)*

Feasting and excellence were part of the Party Rules that the Lord stressed when He gave us these instructions in Scripture twice, with 1,000 years in-between. His heart did not change towards His people. Remember well, rejoice always, and feast in extravagance in moments of celebration.

Hearts Rekindled

One of the outcomes of healthy celebration is personal renewal. It's the natural response when remembrance and thanksgiving are precursors. There is no way you and I could remember the goodness of God, with thanksgiving and joy in our hearts, and then not go on in re-committing our lives with Him.

In verse 12 of our Deuteronomy passage, Moses instructs the people to remember where they had come from, and to remember the deliverance of the Lord out of it. He encourages them, "When you get together remember the Lord's goodness in bringing you out of bondage. When you get together, be aware of the good things He's done in your life and, when you do, you will be watchful to continue in His ways."

> *And you shall [earnestly] remember that you were a slave in Egypt, and* ***you shall be** **watchful and obey these statutes.***
>
> *Deuteronomy 16:12 (AMPC)*

The phrase 'you shall be' is not a command. It is a description of what takes place in response to right remembering. When our hearts are turned towards Him in our memories, with thanks for His good hand in our lives, this will inspire us to keep our ways before Him in willing surrender.

A commitment to God, to His statutes and His word, is not a hard work of striving. When my heart is free-spirited, grounded in His goodness and my thanksgiving, when I remember the goodness of God, my heart longs to respond and reciprocate. When my heart is filled with the joy of thanksgiving, it longs to come into greater commitment and covenant with Him again.

The phrase 'take care lest you forget' became apparent to me as I re-read the book of Deuteronomy recently. I had never really noticed it before. Yet, as I read Deuteronomy again this time, the repetition of the words 'take care' were jumping off the page at me, chapter after chapter.

Understanding the context, I could see the Lord setting up the ordinances, and way of living for His people, through Moses' leadership and, as this man of God scripted the values and codes for living, he also inserted words of warning. Moses' warning was against the forgetful tendencies which release the heart to wandering.

He said things like, take care lest you forget what you've seen (Deut 4:9). Take care lest you forget the promises and the covenants that bind you with the Lord (Deut 4:23). Take care lest you forget His Words and His statutes (Deut 8:11-14). Take care unless you forget his provision (Deut 11:3-15, 8:17-18). The theme continues again and again. To invert his warning is an acknowledgement that right remembering keeps us in *commitment, covenant and continued connection.* To forget is detrimental, but to remember and renew brings about our success and flourishing.

When I remember that the Lord is good, I want to remain in that place of connection with Him. I want to walk in His ways, to live by His principles, to submit under His beautiful authority, to connect with His promises, and to seek His direction for my life. In remembering God's goodness, we naturally find ourselves recommitting ourselves to Him again. When we take the time to pause and celebrate who He is, we are moved deeply, moved by His love, and we find ourselves bending the knee of our hearts yet again, surrendering to His ways.

Out of sight is often out of mind. However, it is difficult to forget the person standing in front of us. When that person we gaze on, and remember, is the magnificent King of kings, and our precious Jesus, what else is there to do but fall down in surrender again and again?

This is why it is so important to celebrate. Without doing it we forget, become distracted and lured away, we fall away; we fail to renew and recommit. And so, the combination of every memory, and every thanks, becomes a place of commitment, recommitment, and renewal. We should bring our celebration to this end. In itself, celebration is not the end, it is a means to the greater end – ongoing communion and intimacy with Him. Our hearts are rekindled in the joy of remembering Him through celebration.

Homes Of Heaven

At 12 years of age, from a non-English-speaking broken home, I was introduced to a Christian community, and a new way of living. I was quickly befriended by a bubbly dark-haired girl. She was funny and charismatic, affectionate and deeply secure in herself, and in her God. I immediately recognised she was somebody I could ask questions of, and let down my guard with.

Etched into my memory are a number of occasions from my encounters with her, and her family. Particularly the interactions I watched her parents have with each other, and their children, in their home. The house was filled with laughter and practical jokes. Her father was a cheeky, generous, and incurably passionate man. Her mother was a soft-spoken, gentle, elegant woman, with smiling eyes. Her older brother and sister were equally charismatic and fun.

They opened their home to me, and I saw Jesus there.

> *Here's another way to put it: You're here to be light, bringing out the God-colours in the world. God is not a secret to be kept. We're going public with this, as public as a city on a hill. If I make you light-bearers, you don't think I'm going to hide you under a bucket, do you? I'm putting you on a light stand. Now that I've put you there*

on a hilltop, on a light stand – shine! ***Keep open house; be generous with your lives. By opening up to others, you'll prompt people to open up with God, this generous Father in Heaven.***

Matthew 5:16 (MSG)

I distinctly remember my friend's father kissing his wife affectionately, as he made her morning coffee in the kitchen. The way his two daughters tucked in under his arm, and he tickled them or kissed them on their foreheads. I remember sitting around the table at dinner with them for the first time, when they bowed their heads to say Grace together. I have to admit I didn't bow my head or close my eyes. I watched them with sheer amazement at what was taking place before me. My experience in their household transformed my entire being. It was a window into a room I didn't even know existed, but the moment I had caught a glimpse, my heart was convinced that this was the hope for my future. I was determined to create a home where the Lord would be centre.

My pastors were the same when they invited our little family into their home to join the discipleship group they hosted there. Again and again, I could not believe my eyes, as Christian families interacted with each other. I saw the beauty of a thriving marriage, where both spouses lived laid down lives of sacrifice and deference for each other. Meal times were just different. The atmosphere and conversation placed an ache in my heart. My sisters and I were inspired in those spaces. They were places of refuge, to be healed and set on our feet.

You see, God's plan for family time and celebration is that it would be an outreach, and a witness to those who need hope, kindness and support. We don't need to be preachers or famous evangelists, we just need to open our lives.

You shall rejoice before the L*ORD your God,* ***you and your son and your daughter, your male servant and***

> ***your female servant, the Levite who is within your gates, the stranger and the fatherless and the widow who are among you,*** *at the place where the LORD your God chooses to make His name abide. And you shall remember that you were a slave in Egypt, and you shall be careful to observe these statutes. "You shall observe the Feast of Tabernacles seven days, when you have gathered from your threshing floor and from your winepress. And you shall rejoice in your feast,* ***you and your son and your daughter, your male servant and your female servant and the Levite, the stranger and the fatherless and the widow, who are within your gates.****"*
>
> *Deuteronomy 16:11-14 (NKJV)*

This is an all-inclusive affair. Family, friends, employees, strangers, foreigners, the destitute, and the displaced. Our homes reflect God's all-inclusive posture to humanity, and His heart towards everybody.

There is an old Eastern European tradition, where families prepare a spare setting around the table on special occasions. When they ask who the empty place is set for, children are told it is for the stranger who may arrive unexpectedly at our door. It's a beautiful gesture, and builds something of curiosity and social awareness into the hearts of the next generation. But it needs to be more than a gesture. Those seats need to be filled.

I was one of the people who filled a seat like that. I was welcomed in with open arms. I inconvenienced a family. I intruded on their personal and private space. I ate their food, used their toothpaste, and stretched out their bedding on a mattress that would fill an awkward space in their home. They did that for me. And my life was changed. They were quite simply living the Scriptures, but their influence on my life has had a ripple effect beyond anything any of us could have known then.

Through the transformative experiences I had in those homes, a conviction was formed deep on the inside. I started to believe and desire that

I could build a home, where my marriage and my children would thrive, and that this place could be a refuge for others. It would be both a temple and a table, where a different kind of worship and awe would be lifted to the Lord.

Perhaps one of the greatest joys of my Christian walk has been around the altar of our family table with people of all generations. Where meals are shared, questions are asked, prayer is offered, tears are shed, stories are told, laughter echoes after the children running around, in the midst of Heavenly community. As a family, our open home has restored sight and hope to so many who return to offer thanks. Hearts confessing that they were touched in our home the same way mine was touched in the homes of those generous Christians in my early years.

This is the opportunity we have when we build homes of generosity and hospitality. Homes that can call out to a generation, and say come, eat with us, drink with us, learn to live in the way of insight. What beautiful places of discipleship our homes become.

The fifth and final rule of God's Party Etiquette is that it is relational, communal, and inclusive. It inconveniences the private spaces of our lives, to open eternity up in the hearts of others. It is essential that we reclaim the discipline of celebration if for this reason alone. Our generation is starving to be welcomed into homes that look like Heaven.

Celebrating Loss

Perhaps now a very specific, if not niche, discussion to be had for those families who have, or will one day, suffer loss within their family unit. The family the Lord has built for me, in the second half of my life, has been formed out of tragic loss. My exceptionally kind and generous husband, Jared, is my second husband. I am his second wife. We both lost our spouses to cancer in the same year. We both had young children. We had both been in ministry with our late spouses. We both loved the Lord, and have consecrated our whole lives to his service. Jared's late wife, Karen, passed within 18 months of diagnosis, and my husband, Sam, passed within 14 months of diagnosis. They both held faith right up until their final breaths.

We led our children in the walk of prayer, petition, intercession, and travail. Both Jared and I were members of stunning communities of faith who also prayed and prayed and prayed for healing, but it was not to be the way we expected it to be. Jared nursed Karen in the privacy of their own home. I said my goodbyes at Sam's bedside in an intensive care unit. Our children have been well acquainted with the pangs of death. They have seen the clutches of disease ravish their most precious ones, and they have cried out to God.

Jared's girls were 15, four, and two on the morning that they laid flowers on the still frail form of their sweet mother. My girls were 16 and 14, the boys were 12 and 10 when I woke them on my return from the hospital with news that Dad had gone home to be with the Lord. My oldest daughter, Maja, stayed bedside with me in the hospital that night. After watching his final breath, she spent 20 minutes praying for her father to be resurrected, before coming over and embracing me. She was just 16.

I can't remember whether we spoke to each other or not as we drove home from the hospital that night, but we decided that we would wake the other kids to tell them. It was close to midnight. We just knew they may not forgive us if we had waited till the morning to break the news to them. So we got home, woke them all, and sat together in the lounge room.

We chatted for a couple of hours, I answered their questions, we prayed, and went to bed. I will never forget tucking in my beautiful son, Judah, that night. He was only 12 years old at the time. His usual calm demeanour suddenly gave way to an urgent upright seated position in his bed.

"Mum," he gasped. "Can you imagine the sound of Heaven right now as they're reading out Dad's book. Mum, I know we wanted him to be healed, and I know it didn't happen the way we wanted, but I always knew he would be healed either way. He won!"

Over the next weeks each one of my children made their own confessions of revelation about the eternal, about Heaven, about the security, and the confidence that the Lord had shared with them. Together, we made a decision to adopt celebration as the leading posture of our grief. Again the Lord was leading with His divine strategy, and providing celebration as the pathway to healing. I had never before considered a posture of celebration in the face of tragedy and loss, but I can tell you, from my own testimony, that it is the way we overcome.

Marking The Days

> *And the LORD will make you the head and not the tail; you shall be above only, and not be beneath, if you heed the commandments of the LORD your God, which I command you today, and are careful to observe them.*
>
> *Deuteronomy 28:13 (NKJV)*

I quickly realised that each year would bring at least three anniversaries, with the potential to stir up a type of pain that could catch us off guard and linger for days, or even weeks. The days leading up to the date, and the period that followed, could unsettle us if we were unprepared. Every birthday, every anniversary of his passing, and every Father's Day, had the power to be either deeply painful, or to be moments of meaningful honour and reflection that could strengthen us instead. I wanted to be proactive. I wanted to teach my children to recognise the goodness of the Lord, even in the midst of pain. I wanted to equip them. I knew I had to make a plan.

When Jared and I married, those dates immediately doubled to six recurring commemorative events every year in the life of our family. We knew that without a strategic plan to fortify our children, they would quickly become susceptible to the repetitive waves of unrestrained pain. Both Sam and Karen led phenomenal victorious lives in Jesus, and that is the way we wanted them to be remembered and celebrated by their children. That is their legacy.

Jared and I sat together as a new couple, and we made a plan. Then we brought our children on the journey. On the anniversary of their passing each year we have determined to gather together as a family of nine to celebrate these remarkable lives. On that day we prepare what was their favourite meal and dessert, and share it together that night. Afterwards we have the tradition of remembering specific things from their lives.

Jared and the girls go through a memory box of handwritten notes and memories, from family and friends, that were collected at Karen's memorial service. The girls read out loud how Karen was remembered by the people who loved her. As they do so they remember her character in nature, and who she was to the people around her. Her legacy is sown into her daughters again and again, as each card is read out.

We all remember Sam by sitting together in the media room, and watching one of Sam's many preaching videos that still exists on YouTube. It's powerful for the family to watch a man preach the word of God, and pour out his character through the convictions he held so resolutely. We are especially blessed to have those video signatures to be able to go back to. It's both confronting and inspiring at the same time.

They were remarkable people and their legacy deserves to live on, especially in the lives of their children. On their birthdays, the relevant parent pulls the specific children aside in the morning for either a breakfast date and/or a small handwritten card or gift. We celebrate their birthday with the original family unit, rather than the whole family of nine.

And, on Father's Day and Mother's Day, we choose to look outward, and thank God for the spiritual fathers and mothers that the Lord has graciously provided in our community. The kids serve in the Sunday Church gatherings on those days with a sense of privilege and tenacity. They intentionally choose to look at the goodness of God in the land of the living, rather than withdraw and excuse themselves from the day's celebrations out of self-pity and grief. They will call grandfathers and grandmothers. They will honour father-figures and mother-figures in the community, and they will celebrate their adopted father and mother in a way that gives thanks to the Lord for remaining to be kind, on a day where fathers and mothers are esteemed.

It was only a few months after Sam went home to be with the Lord that my 40th birthday rolled around. The last thing I wanted to do was celebrate, but I have two stunning girlfriends who refused to let that milestone pass. They booked a trip for us to the beautiful Whitsunday Islands, off Australia's east coast, and we spent a glorious week in the sunshine, with pristine crystal waters and white sandy beaches. I also laughed so much that my sides hurt. I cried as the beauty and majesty of that creation connected me with the Maker. That week there were moments where the Lord started to breathe new air in my lungs. On the flight home, I heard a whisper in my heart, which I wrote on the back of my boarding pass that sits in my Bible to this day: 'There are a lifetime of memories yet ahead of you'.

This is true. This is our portion in the Lord. His mercies are new every morning and, as the Sun continues to rise, so does His goodness rise upon us. We must choose to celebrate and give thanks.

> *Today I have given you the choice between life and death, between blessings and curses. Now I call on Heaven and Earth to witness the choice you make. Oh, that you would choose life, so that you and your descendants might live!*
>
> *Deuteronomy 30:19 (NLT)*

We always have both options before us, and the Lord tells us which to choose. Even in the face of death, I have learned that I can choose life. Life is a choice. Joy is a choice. And the joy of the Lord is my strength. It's a choice towards a new default. It's intentional. He turns my mourning into dancing, and He gives me a garment of praise for a spirit of heaviness. He's clear on what His preferred wardrobe is for me. Biblical mourning is beautiful and essential. Soulish sorrow is not; soulish sorrow is a spiral that doesn't lead anywhere good. Biblical mourning is hope-filled.

> *And now, dear brothers and sisters, we want you to know what will happen to the believers who have died so you will not grieve like people who have no hope. For since we believe that Jesus died and was raised to life again, we also believe that when Jesus returns, God will bring back with him the believers who have died.*
> *1 Thessalonians 4:13-14 (NLT)*

Mourning, while it is essential, is not the Lord's intended landing place for me. Neither is a spirit of heaviness His preferred wardrobe for me.

> *You have turned my mourning into joyful dancing.*
> *You have taken away my clothes of mourning and clothed me with joy.*
> *Psalm 30:11 (NLT)*

> *To console those who mourn in Zion,*
> *To give them beauty for ashes,*
> *The oil of joy for mourning,*
> *The garment of praise for the spirit of heaviness;*
> *That they may be called trees of righteousness,*
> *The planting of the LORD, that He may be glorified.*
> *Isaiah 61:3 (NKJV)*

The milestones kept rolling around. A few months after my 40th birthday would have been my 20th wedding anniversary. As I saw the date approaching, I wondered how I could turn this into a celebration of thanks. I remembered that Sam always used to talk about designing a family crest, and so I decided on what would have been my 20th wedding anniversary, instead of receiving a gift or a piece of jewellery from my husband who had gone home to be with the Lord, I would give a gift to each of our four children.

I commissioned a master craftsman jeweller in Adelaide, Australia, to design a family crest for us with the elements that Sam would often talk about – the Lion of the tribe of Judah, the flame of the Holy Spirit, and the anatomic heart of God's love for humanity. The jeweller then custom-made four individual signet rings, and engraved each crest by hand into the gold. While the same, they are each uniquely different because they were each hand-crafted and engraved.

On the date of the anniversary, I took the children away for a couple of nights to one of our favourite retreats near Noosa, on the Sunshine Coast of Queensland. I took them to an upmarket restaurant with white tablecloths, and polished silverware. After the main course was cleared from the table, I presented them with four beautiful wooden boxes, and braced myself for their reactions. They cradled the boxes and slowly lifted the lids in unison. Their faces were filled with joy, which turned to awe, which turned to a well of tears, and tear-stained cheeks. They looked at me, and then back at their rings, in silence. Yet again I realised how formative and healing intentional celebration truly can be. Yet again I realised that life is a choice, and celebration is a pathway to it.

Grief Redeemed

Possibly the best advice I received in those dark, dark nights of the soul, was from my pastor, Leigh Ramsey.

"Don't ask why, honey. Why does not have an answer right now. Instead ask, what now? What now always has an answer."

This became my minute by minute, hour by hour, day by day mantra.

What now?

Get out of bed.

What now?

Brush your teeth and make breakfast for your kids.

What now?

Put the washing on.

What now?

Send a message of appreciation to that person who blessed you yesterday.

What now?

I was amazed that the Lord would very quickly put me on my feet, and turn me outwards again. I found that, in His order of doing things, the best way to heal was to give myself away. It is the Gospel message. It is the model of Saviour Jesus.

In our time of loss, Jared and I both independently committed to continued lives of devotion to Jesus, even beyond the grave. We continued, the way we always had, in living our lives for His purposes. Today we are absolutely amazed at the way that the Lord has used our story as encouragement to so many people around the world. Only the Lord can turn around a story like that – turn what looks like evil and make it good. But it is His signature after all, isn't it?

> *And we know that all things work together for good to those who love God, to those who are the called according to His purpose.*
>
> *Romans 8:28 (NKJV)*

Sam went home to be with the Lord on Passover Thursday night. The night, when the spirit of death is literally meant to pass over, was the night when my husband went home to be with the Lord. We stayed home the next day, Good Friday, and one of our assistant pastors delivered the news to the Church that their pastor had graduated to Heaven the night before. On the evening of Silent Saturday, I asked the children whether they wanted to go to the services on Sunday morning – Resurrection Sunday. They looked at me as though I was speaking in another language. Unanimously, they insisted that, of course, it was the only place we would be.

On the drive to the Church building on Easter Sunday morning, I explained to the children that we would enter quietly through a backdoor, and possibly leave early depending on how they were all feeling. Upon arrival we were incredibly overwhelmed with the sense of family in the room that day. Enveloped in love and shared grief by the ones who had walked the journey with us. The service was beautiful, and the children stood by my side on the front row, expecting to leave immediately after the service.

I asked them if they wanted to stay back, and watch the water baptisms which take place as a tradition every year on Resurrection Sunday. They all agreed that they wanted to stay – these days are always the most joyous occasions of the Church calendar, with scores of people making a public declaration of faith, dying to the old, and rising again a new creation through the waters of baptism. It felt so fitting to watch the power of resurrection in people's lives today.

As we stood watching each beautiful person go through the waters of baptism, we celebrated with applause and worship and prayer. With each new testimony that was spoken, my heart began to heal. As I looked down the line of people readying themselves to go into the baptismal waters, my eyes stopped with one particular young man. He looked green with heartache. This particular young man had been to healing crusades with Sam. He had done detox plans, and diet regimes, with Sam. He had been a source of moral support. I remembered how he had told us that he was looking forward to being baptised by Sam when he had recovered. As he stood at the back of the queue today, he looked more alone than anyone in the whole world.

I started to cry, and asked my assistant to get word to him immediately. I watched her weave her way through the crowd and whisper in his ear, "Would you like Karolina to jump in the tank and baptise you today?" He looked up at me from the distance, and nodded. I quickly went to find some appropriate clothes for jumping into a tank of water, and made my way back in time for his turn. I apologised that it wasn't what either of us had hoped, but that the Lord was with us in our Plan B all the same. As we baptised him, and wept together, the Lord spoke so clearly to me with a prophetic word for this friend.

It was after that day that I remembered the powerful Scripture in Philippians 1:21.

> *For to me, to live is Christ, and to die is gain. But if I live on in the flesh, this will mean fruit from my labour; yet what I shall choose I cannot tell. For I am hard-pressed between the two, having a desire to depart and be with Christ, which is far better. Nevertheless to remain in the flesh is more needful for you.*
> *Philippians 1:21-24 (NKJV)*

Some go on ahead of us to be with the Lord, while we still remain. For those of us who remain, there is still so much more that needs to be done here. To live in Christ – and to live in Christ is to give oneself away. There are miracles in that.

Seven days after Sam went home to be with the Lord, I received a text message from one of the young women in our Church community who was midterm in her pregnancy. We had walked closely with this beautiful soul over the years since her radical salvation and transformation in Jesus. We officiated the wedding between her and her young husband. But this text message pierced my heart. She was telling me that the baby had been lost, and she would have to deliver a stillborn child in the morning.

I offered to go to the delivery room with her, and be with her in that process. Fully aware of the recent loss in our family, she reluctantly explored that prospect, and admitted that she would love to have my presence with her through the labour and delivery. I absolutely and resolutely knew that there was no other place that I was supposed to be that day than by her side.

I've been present for many births. Usually those moments are filled with joy and anticipation, because the pain of childbirth has a deep sense of excitement for what is about to come – new life and new beginnings. The delivery room for this child had quite a different atmosphere to it. Grief filled the room, as I watched this beautiful couple worship and pray through the induction, and the contractions, and the delivery, knowing that they would be embracing the lifeless form of their first child within moments. The sound of her deep moan at the final push still rings in my ears.

When the little girl had been born, she was swaddled in blankets and placed in her mother's arms who, by now, had delicately reclined into the bed. I watched this new father and mother lean into each other as they wept. After a short while, he brought the little baby over to me, and placed her body in my arms. So tiny. At that moment the doctor and midwife left the room, and the sound of the worship which had been playing softly in the background all day somehow came to the fore and filled the room.

This beautiful young mother, who is one of the worship leaders in our Church, began to sing out loud the lyrics to the song which was playing. I felt Heaven come into the room. I thought to myself, "Now this is worship". Her beautiful voice pierced the darkness, and defied death with a song of exultant contrite worship to the King of Kings, the God who she loved in life, and still loved now in death.

I stood there in a place that felt other-worldly, as though I was somehow standing between Earth and Heaven itself. For a moment I felt that the veil had been pulled back. With the sound of her mother's voice filling the room, while I held this tiny baby in my arms, I suddenly had a vision. I saw Sam on the other side, healthy and alive, holding who I knew to be this little girl in his arms, also healthy and alive.

The midwife entered the room again. The world came rushing back in. The moment was over. But I will never forget how supernatural that day was. I had every reason to stay home that day, to avoid another hospital room, to shield myself from pain, and to turn away from confronting difficult realities.

But I knew I did not want to live that way, not then, not in that moment. I chose to respond to the invitation of Heaven, and to stand with a beautiful friend who had become family. I am so grateful that I did. It reflects a principle I have learned through this journey of grief and celebration. The principle is this: we can only begin to reconcile the irreconcilable by giving it away.

SECTION FOUR

Reclaim & Rest

GARDENS OF THE HEART

In 2013, we moved our young family from one side of town to the other. My husband and I had responded to an invitation, from the Lord and our senior pastors, to take on one of the locations of our multi-site Church. We move from the south side of Brisbane to the north side, in a coastal peninsula area called Redcliffe. At the time we had three young children, and I was pregnant with our fourth.

We did a season of living between the two hemispheres of our city, as we gradually moved our lives north. The children stayed in school on the southside until there was an opening closer to where we were establishing our new lives, and finally both our school girls were in a school together on the northside of Brisbane.

Our second daughter, Layla, was excited about her new school. We bought an antique desk for her bedroom which we found online. It was an original timber schoolhouse desk. With the flip top desk and bench seat, all attached as one unit. I would estimate it dating back to the early 1900s. The old inkwell was still carved into the top corner of the desk, and decades of etched engravings into the timber flip top lid surface were the playground of imagination for our young girl.

Early in that new school year her class went on an excursion to a place called Petrie Old Town. She had always been a bubbly expressive child, so I was excited to hear her recount of the day's adventure. Tucking her into bed that night, she was bursting to tell me about her experiences of the day.

"Mum! Did you know that Churches were gardens?" Big blue eyes behind her curtain of white blonde hair tossed over the pillow, as she blurted out this question. I had to ask her to explain what she meant.

"Mum, at Old Town the Church was a garden. Instead of seats there were rows of grass. There was no roof. And instead of a pulpit there was a big rock boulder." I could see her imagination had been captivated and set alight.

Over the coming days, as I continued to think about this revelation she had, it began to unravel in my own life. Yes – Layla was right, Churches really are gardens, and those gardens are our hearts, waiting to be cultivated. To steal away to regularly. To meet with our King and Father in the garden Churches of our hearts.

This meditation progressed. An idea of rest. An idea of inner calm. Truly, there is no rest until I know myself, and I cannot know myself until I know my Maker. Real rest comes from a place of identity, and identity is rooted in origin.

We live in a generation that is thirsty for rest, and peace, and calm. Spiritual retreats are booked out. Hobbies and entertainment fill our lives, and empty our bank accounts. Travel plans and bucket lists are go-to Band-Aid solutions for hectic and empty lives. None of them are innately bad. It's just that they are not true rest. They're only counterfeits, and placebos, for the rest we so desperately crave.

He has also set eternity in the human heart.
Ecclesiastes 3:11 (NIV)

And so I began to explore the concept of rest. What is true rest? When did it start? How did it start? To answer these questions I had to go all the way back to Eden. The garden. The first garden.

Hearts Of Dust

Piercing the clouds, a celestial Hand reaches out of Heaven, and dips His miraculous fingers into the dirt of the Earth. He gathers, He shapes, He gives physical form to the yearning of His heart. A body… of dust.

Glorious Creator draws near, ever closer, leaning over the clay. He breathes into the nostrils of that humble yet magnificent countenance.

Searing pain of first-drawn breath into virgin lungs brings body, soul, spirit to life.

Perfection. Splendour. Glory.

And in six days all that has been made was made, and the beautiful declaration sung over it was that it was good; indeed it was very good.

And what was it that the Creator would do on the day after He had completed His creation on the seventh day? He rested, not because he was tired. I doubt our Lord gets tired. No, he rested. Not because He was tired, but because He wanted to spend time with His beloved.

> *By the seventh day God had finished the work He had been doing; so on the seventh day He rested from all His work.* ***Then God blessed the seventh day and made it holy****, because on it He rested from all the work of creating that He had done.*
> *Genesis 2:2-3 (NIV)*

It was the first ever holy day, the origins of our word holiday. It was a day of rest, a Sabbath. God established a rhythm to this day, where He would visit with man and woman. He would walk with them in the cool of the day, in unbroken perfect communion. He had a habit, and rhythm, of visiting with man and woman.

This first Sabbath was not just rest in the sense of laying back and doing nothing. Sabbath was holy because it was a time of connection between God and mankind. This is what I realised rest truly should be.

It was not long before the fall and the separation between God and man. When that deceitful forked tongue whispered the devastating lie into the ear of God's beloved. Taking the bait, man and woman surrendered their derived authority, their dominion, and their communion. They were reefed violently away from their Creator, their Father, their Source, their origin, and thrown into the strenuous realities of a world absent from rest.

Pervading God's people, Israel – and indeed, all of humanity – was the ache of longing to find rest again, true rest. The God of Abraham, Isaac and Jacob began to whisper words of promise over His people. *I'm going to bless you, not on your merits but just because I love you. This blessing can only be received through faith, no sense of striving or works, just faith.*

Two and a half thousand years passed between Adam and Moses. Between the first pattern of rest and the second. Where the first pattern of rest was etched on hearts of dust, the second would be etched on hearts of stone.

Hearts Of Stone

In and out of slavery. Four hundred years under the rule of Egypt. Whipped and marred and battered and bruised, generation after generation. The cry of the people reaches the ears of God, and He eventually raises up a deliverer, a man named Moses, who leads them out of Egypt by a miraculous series of events.

They are now free people, marching in the wilderness on their way to a land that God promised their forefathers, thousands of years ago. After months of weary travelling, they come to the foot of a mountain called Sinai, the place most famous for where God gave the 10 Commandments, carved into stone tablets.

Moses is their leader, and also the mediator between God and His people. The people were comfortable with that. A middle man, someone who could meet with this fearfully awe-inspiring God on their behalf. They ask

Moses to go to God, and ask Him for a list of rules to live by. It is one of the great shortcomings of our frail natures, to prefer a checklist, a set of rules, a code rather than the connection of heart and accountability of relationship.

God did not want to pass down a law. He had always preferred the covenant He established with their forefathers. He wanted them to remain in a covenant relationship with Him, but it is just like humanity to prefer a list than a relationship. It's easier to meet a criterion than to be accountable. It's easier to dot 'i's and cross 't's than it is to be vulnerable. A contract feels safer than a covenant.

So they asked Moses to ask God for a box they could fit into. Reluctantly the Lord obliged and passed down 10 laws.

Exodus 20: 1-17

1. You shall have no other gods before me
2. You shall not make idols
3. You shall not take the name of the Lord your God in vain
4. You shall remember the Sabbath day and keep it holy
5. Honour your father and mother
6. You shall not murder
7. You shall not commit adultery
8. You shall not steal
9. You shall not be false witness against your neighbour
10. You shall not covet

There is a remarkable conviction calling out to us from this list. When you see it, you'll never unsee it again. Look more closely at the first four of the 10. What are those first four calling us to? He didn't want to give us the Law but, even when it came down to it, He instituted relationship in the first four of the 10. What do they reveal? They reveal His desperate longing for us.

Don't forget me.

Don't replace me.

I just want to be with you.

I'm jealous of your time.

I'm jealous of your affection.

Please remember me.

Please always come back and spend time with me

And number four, the most beautiful: remember this Sabbath day and keep it holy. Remember that time when we walked together in the cool of the day. Remember that time before the separation when we were in unbroken communion together daily, weekly, and in all the rhythms of life.

And so the nation of Israel receives this new code to live by, and they continue the journey towards their place of Promise. Always falling short, always missing the mark. Always close, yet not close enough. But another deliverer was coming Who would bring the restitution and redemption, and all that was lost at the fall.

It was 1,500 years between the deliverer, Moses, and this ultimate deliverer, Jesus. In that time, Israel turned 10 Commandments into 613 laws – the painful symptoms of a human nature obsessed with work. Obsessed with the over-glorification of busy. It's not a new thing. It's the fallen human condition.

There is a difference between the covenant of Grace, and the law of Works.

The covenant of Grace, given to Abraham, Isaac and Jacob, was given in spite of their best efforts – in spite of their lousy, fault-ridden tendencies. They were just as dysfunctional as the rest of us. And yet God promised blessings to their family line. Abraham found favour with God, not because of his works but because of his faith. They were in favour because of Grace, and yet they chose to exchange a covenant of rest for a law of works.

> *The people all responded together, "We will **do** everything the LORD has said." So Moses brought their answer back to the LORD.*
>
> *Exodus 19:8 (NIV)*

While the Lord wanted a covenant of heart, the people constantly referred back to what they would do, and how they would work to gain the His favour. There was one coming who would be the only successful Covenant Keeper on our behalf, to bring us back into that covenant of Grace where our hearts could finally rest from their own hardness, and come back into a place of abiding in our Maker.

Hearts Of Flesh

We find that Jesus turned all the Law on itself; in fact, He was the fulfilment of the Law. Through Him we become living temples. Places of His habitation. Places of His dwelling. Places of His residence.

> *Do you not know that your bodies are temples of the*
> *Holy Spirit, who is in you, whom you have received from*
> *God? You are not your own;*
> *1 Corinthians 6:19 (NIV)*

We now house the very presence of God. What was once restricted to a physical location, a temple, a ritual is now present with us, and among us, and in us. He is so close.

During His time on Earth, we see Jesus Himself withdraw to pray and rest. There, in the quiet places, He connected with the Father.

> *But Jesus often withdrew to lonely places and prayed.*
> *Luke 5:16 (NIV)*

There, in the quiet places, He would walk with God again, just like the first Adam did in the ancient garden. He withdrew to reconnect, to gain understanding, to be strengthened and sharpened. He withdrew to mourn and be comforted. He withdrew to be commissioned, and to find Himself in His Father again. It was a place where Jesus would remember who He was, and who sent Him. It was the place where He denied the noise of the world for the call of Heaven.

> *Very early in the morning, while it was still dark, Jesus got up, left the house and went off to a solitary place, where He prayed.*
> *Mark 1:35 (NIV)*

> *Then Jesus went with his disciples to a place called Gethsemane, and He said to them, "sit here while I go over there and pray."*
> *Matthew 26:36 (NIV)*

> *He went to Nazareth, where He had been brought up, and on the Sabbath Day He went into the synagogue, as was His custom.*
> *Luke 4:16 (NIV)*

Even his custom of going to the synagogue on the Sabbath Day modelled, not a religious ritual, but an expression of relationship. And so we see the progression of rest:

EDEN	SINAI	GETHSEMANE
Hearts of Dust	Hearts of Stone	Hearts of Flesh
Initiated	Legislated	Liberated
Rest	Religion	Relationship
Invitation	Obligation	Restitution

So what of our garden Church, and Layla's timely revelation? I believe the Lord showed me that our hearts are, indeed, like garden Churches, like landscapes; that our inner world is very much like a garden in which we are called to cultivate.

As I lay there beside her small frame on the bed that night, she finished her description with a statement that rang like a bell in my spirit.

"And I do this too," she said.

She drifted off to sleep and I wondered what 'this' actually meant to her. What was it that she was saying she did? I imagined a small child in a garden, waiting to meet with their most Beloved Friend. I imagined myself making my heart a place where Jesus visits with me. A place I cultivate, and I often go to. A place I draw away to, and He meets me there.

I wonder how many Christians have gardens that are neglected and overgrown. Is this the place they go to when they draw away? Is this the place where they meet exclusively with Jesus, where there is no-one else in this place except Him. Where this is the place of solitude and relationship they share with Him alone.

My pondering continued. How would I cultivate this garden? How do I care for this garden Church of my heart?

PROVISION IN THE PROMISED

Being the daughter of two migrant parents, from the earliest age work ethic was taught to me as a life principle. My parents were 19 and 20 when they married, and fled communist Poland. They wanted to offer their future family the kinds of opportunities they couldn't see being offered in their homeland.

At the time, Canada and Australia were the two prospective options available. They chose Australia because my father had seen a postcard of Surfer's Paradise on the Gold Coast. He figured, to himself, that any nation with colour on its architecture and its billboards, would be a nation of creativity and hope, where people were free. While a simple postcard may have been the inspiration for the selection criteria for an international relocation, the heart of their dream was to access opportunities, and to build a better life.

I was swiftly taught, but there's no such thing as a free lunch. I was told that life would be whatever I made it. I was taught to recognise and maximise opportunities. I was taught to push my own limits, and realise my potential. I was taught to despise complacency, and recognise the greatest limitations would only ever be the ones I place on myself. Quitting was not an option.

At the end of high school, my father made it quite clear that I was required to go to university, and at least achieve a bachelor-level qualification. Anything else I decided to do was optional after this had been completed. They had given up everything, and risked everything, to offer us the life they feared they would never have for themselves. I will forever be grateful for the strength that my parents imparted to me, and the resilience they modelled. As a result, I have always valued work ethic, and I have enjoyed a life of fruitful productivity.

God's pattern for living is one of productivity and rest simultaneously. He invites us to be a people who sacrifice and celebrate. He invites us to be people who are contributors and heirs. We work and we celebrate. We sacrifice and we give thanks. We expend and we rest in regular rhythms.

To be industrious is a part of our design. It's dangerous to be non-productive when we are designed to be like the Father – creative, productive, fruitful. We have His derived authority to make things better in the world. It's who we are. It's our DNA.

> *A slack hand causes poverty, but the hand of the diligent makes rich. He who gathers in summer is a prudent son, but he who sleeps in harvest is a son who brings shame.*
>
> *Proverbs 10:4–5 (ESV)*

Why then has this produced so much pain and dysfunction throughout history, and in our lives today? Why are we exhausted and burnt out? Why the constant drive for more, and more, and more? The desperate and insatiable plight for acquisition? The breakdown of relationships and soul as a result? Where did it come from? And how do we escape?

It all goes back to the first garden. I found that all of life's issues are answered in one of two gardens. Eden or Gethsemane. Where two Adams wrestled. Where one failed, the other prevailed.

But let's go back to Eden only moments after we were given the beautiful ordinance to work in rhythm and fruitfulness. The first Adam, believing the lie, betrayed the heart of his Father. Sinking his teeth into the fruit, and ushering in a new and lesser way of being. The Father addresses the woman, the serpent, and then Adam himself. It's heart wrenching.

Then to Adam He said, "Because you have heeded the voice of your wife, and have eaten from the tree of which I commanded you, saying, 'You shall not eat of it':
"Cursed is the ground for your sake;
In toil you shall eat of it
All the days of your life.
Both thorns and thistles it shall bring forth for you,
And you shall eat the herb of the field.
In the sweat of your face you shall eat bread
Till you return to the ground,
For out of it you were taken;
For dust you are,
And to dust you shall return."
Genesis 3:17-19 (NKJV)

The work is not taken away, but its effectiveness and its outcomes are. Certainly the benefits of work transform into laboursome toil and devastating lack. What was once fruitful and abundant, becomes inferior and never enough.

After Adam, humanity continued for generations in this pattern, following that exchange in the garden. Generations of toil and struggle. The Lord's people find themselves in captivity, in a land called Egypt, under a slave driver named Pharaoh.

Four hundred years of forced hard labour. The ever-increasing and endless burden on the backs of people, who could never satisfy the quotas and demands. As they moaned under the weight, the Lord heard their cry. Raising up Moses to deliver them into their own land, and into their own way of being a covenant people, to learn a new way. He was calling them into the Promised Land – and He would teach them His provision, if they would listen.

It is still the same today. We draw a distinct correlation between the pattern of the world, and the pattern of Egypt. One of work, and toil, and slavery. And today the Lord is still calling us into a land of plenty, as He was then. A place of rest and provision. Where work has a rhythm and rest is a state of the heart. Our Salvation into the family of God symbolises us leaving the world and its systems, and an entering into the Promised Land of the Kingdom of Heaven.

Sabbath rest strengthens our relationship with God, and enables us to live in alignment with His design, not in a cycle of constant striving. A few years ago our Church received a prophetic promise through David McDonald, who is a father in the faith and one of the founding fathers of our denomination.

> *You are coming into a season of breakthrough in finances," he began. "If we don't then God's people will stay in poverty tied to the world's systems. We have got to tie ourselves to God's system. We will serve God's system and see miracles.*
>
> *David McDonald*

There are two systems – that of the world, and that of the Kingdom of Heaven. Walter Brueggmann writes beautifully on the Egypt concept, and what a life of rest now looks like in the promises of God. He explains that when we align ourselves with the Kingdom of Heaven, we step away from the systems of the world, with their pressures and demands. At that moment, Pharaoh no longer rules over us, and we are no longer the sole source of our own provision. There was much to unlearn as we entered a new system, and a new Kingdom.

The Lord began to speak to us about the idea of rest, and our invitation to enter into it. It seemed to be a central theme on His heart. Yet to embrace what He desired for us, we had to let go of the patterns of the world – a system without rest, where there was never enough. A system where we were compelled to work constantly to produce more. Where hierarchy and competition dictated interactions, and everyone was guarding themselves while keeping an eye on others. We were striving to keep up with our neighbours at best and, at worst, taking advantage of them.

He didn't just ask us to rest from all that, He insisted on it. Why? What was he trying to teach us? Here lies the deepest truth that we must conceive, and bring to bear in our lives, if we are to live lives of rest and promise.

The Lord is my source now. He is my provider.

Like Abraham on Mount Moriah, in His provision, I come to learn His name and nature as Jireh, my provider. The Sabbath recognises God as the Source. Not the world. Not self. Not a system, a boss or another person. The Sabbath recognises God as Source.

Over and over throughout both Testaments, the Lord speaks about the hardness of heart that takes people out of rest. He literally equates hardness of heart with an absence of rest. That has gravity. When you insist on being your own source, your own provider, you harden your heart towards God. When a heart is hardened towards the Lord, it is the most restless.

We must adequately and fully unpack this reality in our lives. We must reach deep into the guidance of the Spirit of God, to learn the beautiful pattern for living that the Lord would have for us as a blessing. It's a layered journey.

Let's revisit the fourth commandment about Sabbath, and look at it a little bit more closely.

> *Remember to observe the Sabbath day by keeping it holy. You have six days each week for your ordinary work, but the seventh day is a Sabbath day of rest dedicated to the LORD your God. On that day no one in your household may do any work. This includes you, your sons and daughters, your male and female servants, your livestock, and any foreigners living among you. For in six days the LORD made the heavens, the Earth, the sea, and everything in them; but on the seventh day he rested. That is why the LORD blessed the Sabbath day and set it apart as holy.*
>
> *Exodus 20:8-11 (NLT)*

Six days of industrious work, and one day of Sabbath rest every week. Let's slow down and look at the various elements of this precept.

Industry and productivity are neither things to run from, nor things to be obsessed with. Quite simply, industry and productivity are healthy states for our beings to enjoy. At the very beginning of time, at creation itself, the Lord gave us an ordinance for industry and productivity. He released us to a life of fruitfulness, multiplication, dominion, and authority.

> *So God created man in His own image; in the image of God He created him; male and female He created them. Then God blessed them,* ***and God said to them, "Be fruitful and multiply; fill the Earth*** *and subdue it; have dominion over the fish of the sea, over the birds of the air, and over every living thing that moves on the Earth."*
>
> *Genesis 1:27-28 (NKJV)*

Again, in the second chapter of Genesis, we read it in a beautiful way relating specifically to the garden itself. That he put the man into His creation with the purpose of working it, and keeping it.

> *The LORD God took the man and put him in the garden of Eden to* ***work it and keep it****.*
>
> *Genesis 2:15 (ESV)*

It is an ordinance of man to work, keep, cultivate, improve and make better the world around him. Work is a healthy state of being. Even Jesus invited us into a place of work. His invitation is breathtaking.

> *Are you tired? Worn out? Burned out on religion? Come to Me. Get away with Me and you'll recover your life. I'll show you how to take a real rest. Walk with*

> *Me and work with Me – watch how I do it. Learn the unforced rhythms of grace. I won't lay anything heavy or ill-fitting on you. Keep company with Me and you'll learn to live freely and lightly.*
>
> *Matthew 11:28-30 (MSG)*

I invite you to study that passage in all of the different translations. According to Jesus, work and burden are not evil, as some teaching suggests these days. I regret that some false teaching has condemned works entirely as legalism, and it has quietly eroded people's sense of responsibility, diligence, and fruitfulness. I've seen too many deconstruct their commitment to the Church, and to service, in the Kingdom. The fruit is never good.

Let us be clear. A driven work ethic, lacking communion and dependence on the Lord, is the very thing the Lord regretted in His people more than anything else. This leads to places of exhaustion and burnout.

At the other end of the spectrum is the lazy and slothful person. One who was not playing their part. One who Proverbs warns against becoming. One who is not meeting the divine potential, knitted into the very fibre of their being.

The work itself is not the question – that is a given. What must be resolved is who assigns that work, and the way in which it's carried out. The motive behind it. Who receives the credit for it. Its origins and purposes. The why behind the what, and the Who behind the why.

> *I have been crucified with Christ and I no longer live, but Christ lives in me. The life I now live in the body, I live by faith in the Son of God, who loved me and gave Himself for me.*
>
> *Galatians 2:20 (NIV)*

My life is not my own. I was purchased with a price. The precious Blood of Jesus Himself ransomed my life. He has a plan for me. He formed me in my mother's womb. He fashioned me intentionally with unique gifts, talents, and abilities. He intended the personality I have. Everything about this life I live is by His design, and His intention. When I come alive to Christ, it is He who lives in me. My life reflects the reality of His provision and His purposes in every way.

He is writing a story. The narrative of humanity past, present, and future. He is looking for willing vessels to bring His Kingdom, here and now, into our experience. It is our commitment to His purposes that will bring more of Heaven to Earth, so that more of Earth can go to Heaven. In all our unique ways, endowed by Him, we play a part in that narrative.

> *You shall remember the Lord your God, for it is He who gives you power to get wealth, that He may confirm His covenant that He swore to your fathers, as it is this day.*
> *Deuteronomy 8:18 (ESV)*

We are simultaneously active and at rest. Rest is the place we *work from, not towards*. Not only does Sabbath recognise the Lord as my Source, but it also puts Him first. It's the principle of firsts, and something I could write an entire other book on.

Why is this important to the Family Altar? Because as long as we live under the whip of the world, we will withhold our children from the Lord. We will continue grooming them, as we were, towards careers and qualifications as priority over the fire of the Spirit within them. Their passionate embers are then quenched before they take full flame. Both are important, but one must come first, and must be the guiding flame. The other follows in its path.

Blessed From The Root

Our lives are an opportunity to give God the first, and the best, in all things. Our lives are an opportunity to worship Him in abandon. Out of an overflow of revelation, our lives are a blessed opportunity to prioritise the things of Heaven. It's only when we do this in purity and truth, that the full blessing and rest become our portion in Him.

When I put myself in the right perspective, when I put the Lord in right perspective, I recognise how feeble my attempts are to provide and elevate my own efforts. When I surrender my priorities to Him, I have finally understood that it was all His anyway. I am finally in a place where I can live from Him, and for Him, again.

In honouring the Sabbath, our families learn that we can do more in six days than the world will strive to do in seven. It's exactly the same principle as the tithe. By giving a tenth, the Christian is blessed and thriving on 90 percent of what the world has. This is a manifestation of the miraculous covenant we have with our God. In exactly the same way my efforts in six days, when a Sabbath is given to the Lord with joy, will far out-produce what my own strength could ever do in seven whole days. It will never make sense to the natural mind. Spiritual things never do. And the flesh continually wages against them.

> *"For My thoughts are not your thoughts,*
> *Nor are your ways My ways," says the* LORD.
> *"For as the heavens are higher than the Earth,*
> *So are My ways higher than your ways,*
> *And My thoughts than your thoughts."*
> *Isaiah 55:8-9 (NKJV)*

Do you remember the Israelites in the wilderness who were relying on manna from the Lord each day? They were clearly told to collect only enough for what their household needed for that day alone. They were told to collect a double portion on the sixth day to make up for the seventh, when they would not go out to collect manna. The Lord didn't want them collecting provision on the day of rest. He would multiply what they collected in the previous days so that they had more than enough to allow for a day of communion and rest with Him.

Those who gathered more than they needed (on days one to five), discovered that their portion of manna would spoil and become inedible. It is a stark illustration, but the principle is clear. I have seen it play out in the lives of colleagues, friends, and many others I have encountered. In their striving, what they acquire and accomplish for themselves often turns sour, with consequences that cannot be undone. Families are fractured, marriages strained, and destinies compromised. A hardened heart cannot enter the rest of God. If only their efforts had been surrendered first to the priorities of Heaven, the outcome would have been entirely different.

This is the Kingdom. This is the covenant. Our surrender is a willing act of obedience and priority. It is the first and the best I have to give. This is my most joyous surrender. I offer the Lord that day of rest and communion, and He blesses the other six days. Because when the first is holy, the rest is holy, and His holiness on my humanness is the Promised Land of the miraculous.

> *If the part of the dough offered as firstfruits is holy, then the whole batch is holy; if the root is holy, so are the branches.*
>
> *Romans 11:16 (NIV)*

My friend, this is the infallible Word of God. He promises us that, if we give Him the first, He will bless the rest. What a wicked deception of the enemy it is that any one of us created beings would presume to take our life into our own hands.

> *Rest is a weapon given to us by God. The enemy hates it because He wants us to be stressed and occupied.*
>
> *Elizabeth Elliot*

The enemy of our souls knows very well what our portion is in the Lord, and he will go to any extreme length to ensure we never get into it. Pride, busyness, distraction, jealousy, are his schemes to diminish us. However, active surrender to the Lord is where we want to live. Where we are fully alive in our design for fruitful and industrious living. Free from the curse of self-sufficiency and toil. This is the Kingdom here now, in my present-day experience. This is what He wanted for us.

> *Therefore do not worry, saying, 'What shall we eat?' or 'What shall we drink?' or 'What shall we wear?' For after all these things the Gentiles seek. For your heavenly Father knows that you need all these things. But seek first the Kingdom of God and His righteousness, and all these things shall be added to you. Therefore do not worry about tomorrow, for tomorrow will worry about its own things. Sufficient for the day is its own trouble.*
> *Matthew 6:31-34 (NKJV)*

Remember, we left the world and its ways, its fears, its dogmas. We died to self, and came alive to Christ. His indwelling Spirit is our constant guide, if we should choose to follow. Now we can understand, with empathy, why it truly is a hard heart that resists this rest. It's a heart that says, "No thanks God, I've got this sorted. I'll take care of it." What an enormous loss, such a grave falling short, being deceived and lacking belief. The Lord is saying, "Give me your first, and I will abundantly care for you. I will walk with you. You will know My voice. You will know My table, My green pastures and still waters. Let Me lead you."

That means turning off the phone. Silencing the rush of the outside world. Pulling away into the quiet places with Him. Bringing our children into those rhythms with us. Protecting them from the whips and deceptive lures of the flesh. We raise them as ones who are prepared for that world, to bring Heaven into it. Rest will be the Promised Land they dwell in.

HEARTHSONGS OF REVERENCE

Learning and teaching the cultivation of the garden, in the heart of the home, has been a beautiful journey. We reclaim those places of rest through very real and practical means. We have found the following disciplines, as priorities to be built into the rhythms of our family life. And when I look at families who are struggling, the marriages that fall apart, the children who walk away from the Lord, usually one or all of these have been missing. A crisis in a family that doesn't happen overnight is generally a very very slow decline, in the wrong direction.

The opposite is also true. Families who thrive are not just lucky, or blessed with good kids or compatible marriages. The families who thrive are the ones who consistently do the right things as a priority. Before all other temptations and distractions, we must build our lives around our priorities, weekly and daily. We decide what is the most important thing, and we build our lives around those things.

We relentlessly come back to what's urgent, over what's important, and we choose to schedule our priorities rather than try to prioritise our schedule. We do the hard things, and make the tough choices, to create the life and family we want. It doesn't come easily. It comes intentionally.

The Word As Home

Every morning, Jared and I open the Word of God together. He has usually returned from the gym and it's about 6am. He has made me a coffee on his return, and brought it into our bedroom. We have two armchairs at the end of the room, and we open the Word of God together. As the children gradually wake one by one, they come into our room and sit on our bed, or on the carpet nearby, sometimes interrupting the flow of our time, often just to say good morning, and to sit in the atmosphere with us for a few moments before they move on with the day. I love that this is the reference point for the start of the day. I know that one day it will be a memory that they treasure – every morning seeing their parents together in the Word of God.

Our children have also developed habits in the Word, some more disciplined than others, but they each have their own rhythm and way of learning Scriptures. As they get older, those rhythms become more established, more disciplined. It gives me great joy to open the door to a room where a dim glow is coming from a quiet space in a bedroom, spying one of my children with the Scripture open late at night before sleep.

I enjoy watching the girls pick special highlighters, and pens, and journals, and create moody spaces for their Bible time every day. The boys have loved spending that time in the mornings. Can I encourage you that your child is not going to drift into this habit, and neither will you? This needs to be a priority that is set, and then arranged.

Meditation is the act of drawing from the deep well of the Word. J I Packer describes it as calling to mind, thinking over, dwelling on, and applying the works, ways and promises of God. It is holy thought, performed consciously in the presence of God, under His eye and by His help, as a means of communion with Him.

God desires to reveal great and hidden things to His people. Meditation positions us to hear His voice, receive His revelation and understand His character. As we meditate, we learn to trust that, if God says He is good, then He is good. If He says that He is faithful, then He is faithful. If He says that He is just, then justice will prevail.

Meditation leads to obedience. We hear the Word and do what it says. It renews the mind, transforms our lives, and strengthens our desire to walk closely with Him.

Throughout Scripture, the men and women used by God were people of meditation. Isaac meditated in the field. Joshua was instructed to meditate day and night. Elijah heard God's whisper. David meditated through the watches of the night. Jesus modelled perfect communion with the Father, hearing and obeying His voice.

Fundamentally I believe the reason our society has broken down to the degree we are seeing today, the reason individuals are so at a loss for meaning, worth, joy, and satisfaction is because we do not know the Word of God.

We are not playing games anymore, friends. No amount of idle time in a Church pew can substitute for personal intimate communion with God. He responds to our seeking Him personally and privately. The Lord rewards those who diligently seek him.

We must know the Holy Scriptures. The Word of God is not something we read once. In fact, you will read those Scriptures every day for the rest of your life. If you love Him, and you are hungry for connection with Him, He reveals Himself through His Holy Scriptures, and we are transformed into His likeness the more we look on Him.

We cultivate the landscape of our hearts by meditating on, and learning, the Word of God. All of it. Too many people are discipled by social media platforms on their devices. Some are well-meaning tools that can be used to our advantage, but they do not replace time in the Holy Scriptures themselves.

We learn the character and nature of God, as we study His interactions with humanity throughout the Scriptures. We learn His intentions, His desires, His will, His promises. We learn the culture of Heaven as He would have it in His people. You and I must devote ourselves to it in all the translations, in all the modes. We must learn the logos Word of God in order to understand His rhema now Word, as we progress through personal circumstances and cultural trends. You will never know Him better than you know His Word.

> *Great peace have those who love Your law,*
> *And nothing causes them to stumble.*
> *Psalm 119:165 (NKJV)*

We are nourished and washed by the word of God as water flowing over us and filling us.

> *Cleansing by the washing with water through the Word.*
> *Ephesians 5:26 (NIV)*

It becomes a bubbling spring that wells up on the inside of us. Just when we need it, the counsel of the Word rises up within us like a well of sweet water – if we have taken the time to dig that well.

> *But whoever drinks the water I give them will never thirst. Indeed, the water I give them will become in them a spring of water welling up to eternal life.*
> *John 4:14 (NIV)*

> *Whoever believes in Me, as Scripture has said, rivers of living water will flow from within them.*
> *John 7:38 (NIV)*

Don't let anyone else read the Word for you. No podcast, no sermon, no small group Bible study leader, is going to be able to dig your well for you. When it really counts, and one day it will, you will need to know the Source for yourself. You will need a wellspring of life to draw from.

Just as the Word is like a bubbling spring of pure water that refreshes and cleanses us, the Scriptures are also substantial bread to sustain us.

> *Jesus answered, "It is written: 'Man shall not live on bread alone, but on every word that comes from the mouth of God.'"*
> *Matthew 4:4 (NIV)*

Jesus himself relied only on the Scripture to refute the enemy's temptation in the wilderness. He didn't rely on His own wisdom, or the wisdom of man. He didn't even rely on his interpretation of Scripture. He simply refused the enemy by quoting Scripture directly in, and of, itself.

In recent years it has grieved me deeply to see people, who have identified as Christians for many years, make decisions that are not aligned with Scripture, and then justify those choices through misinterpretation or distortion of God's Word. Those who commit themselves steadfastly to the truth of Scripture, however, are the ones who are most firmly sustained in their faith.

I always felt as though I would never catch up. I asked my pastor once, "Will I ever unlearn all the faulty mindsets that I grew up with? Will I ever know the Scriptures like the people around me, who seem to be living strong vibrant lives for the Lord?" He taught me that there are aspects of God that are forever to be searched out. That there is no end to the revelation of His majesty, and it would be my lifelong privilege to seek it out.

Eventually, I discovered that the Word is my source of identity. In the book of James we are told that the Scripture is like a mirror, showing us who we are.

> *Do not merely listen to the Word, and so deceive yourselves. Do what it says. Anyone who listens to the Word but does not do what it says is like someone who looks at his face in a mirror and, after looking at himself, goes away and immediately forgets what he looks like. But whoever looks intently into the perfect law that gives freedom, and continues in it – not forgetting what they have heard, but doing it – they will be blessed in what they do.*
> *James 1: 22-25 (NIV)*

I remember reading this passage of Scripture for the first time, and reading it through my faulty lens of condemnation. I thought to myself, "Yeah every time I read the Bible it does show me who I am, and how far I am from the goal".

As I matured in God, and learned more about His nature and His position towards me, I realised that the posture of this Scripture was completely different to what I initially assumed. The truth is that when I read, the Scripture shows me who I truly am in God. It's a reflection of my true nature, and true identity. When I read the Scripture it brings me into my true self, as it does its work in me.

This was not a Scripture to condemn me. No! Quite the opposite. This Scripture was a vote of confidence. A Scripture to reveal the goodness of God within me. So, I approached the Holy Scriptures in a totally different way from that point on. When I read the Word of God, I discover who I really am. I was now looking at myself according to His Word – in the Scriptures I could truly see who I was according to Him. I read the Scriptures, not through condemnation – look how far you are from the mark – but through inspiration of grace – this is who you really are in Me.

> *But because of his great love for us, God, who is rich in mercy, made us alive with Christ even when we were dead in transgressions – it is by grace you have been saved. And God raised us up with Christ and seated us with Him in the heavenly realms in Christ Jesus, in order that in the coming ages He might show the incomparable riches of His grace, expressed in His kindness to us in Christ Jesus.*
> *Ephesians 2:4-7 (NIV)*

As I read the Scriptures, I understand I'm coming into a time of communion with my loving Heavenly Father. It is a time of connection. I am hearing from His heart. His Holy Spirit brings the words to life, and tutors me through them.

I can read the Word of God in the first person, and place myself within the narratives. The Scriptures are unpacked by the Holy Spirit into my everyday life. As I read, I hear His voice. We discuss the things I cannot figure out. I hear His songs over me. I bring my loved ones to Him there, and I am stilled under His voice. I silence the noise, and I learn His intentions.

Families depend on parents who have a deep affection for the Word of God, and who can impart that same hunger into their children. How different the world would be if Christian families held the Holy Scriptures as the centrepiece of their values.

Each time one of our children reached a new stage in their reading development, we marked the milestone by purchasing a new Bible. These moments have been simple yet precious celebrations. The eight-year-old Bible tradition is particularly meaningful. Each child knows that, on their eighth birthday, they will visit the bookstore with Dad and Mum to choose their first 'grown-up' Bible, moving beyond the picture book versions. It is such a joyful time, quietly walking the shelves with them, and helping guide their choice.

I have taken many young people to the Christian bookstore to help them choose a Bible, and often they come from Christian homes, where a Bible had never been provided for them. It is a reminder of how important it is to prioritise the Word of God in our children's lives. Should we, as parents, be more committed to basketball, soccer, football, or dance, than we are of the Word of God in our children's lives? Our actions teach far more than our words, and how we invest in Scripture shapes how our children will value it.

I have found great benefit in reading the Chronological Bible. After many years of studying the conventional Bible, approaching it in chronological order offered a fresh perspective on the Lord. It helped me see Him in a more relational and coherent way, observing how He interacted with humanity over the centuries. I noticed patterns in human nature, and witnessed God's loving and sovereign intervention time and again.

It also helped me understand the mighty men and women of God within the context of their times, which brought a renewed sense of hope for my own generation. Since then, I have continued to read the Chronological Bible regularly in various versions. At first the task of reading the Bible in a year seemed impossible, and I understand that. Yet, when we honestly consider the time we devote to work, entertainment, and other pursuits, it becomes clear how easily our priorities can drift.

In his most exquisite work, called 'Lecture to My Students', Charles Spurgeon is famously quoted as saying:

> *Visit many good books, but live in the Bible.*
> *Charles Spurgeon*

The great evangelist, Billy Graham, reflected on his life this way.

> *If I had to do it over again, I would spend more time in meditation and prayer and just telling the Lord how much I love Him, and I would spend more time studying the Bible and less time traveling.*
> *Billy Graham*

To devote myself to the Scripture, as a priority every day, is to ensure that I will not stumble in and out of seasons. It will ensure that I have the Lord's filter in my decision-making processes. It will secure the prosperity of my family, and the future generations. It must be the primary source of my discipleship, without competition from media content from any other source – Christian or not. I must consume the Word of God directly for myself, every single day, and I must teach my children to do the same.

Woven For Worship

There's a beautiful anticipation and joy in the air of our home on a Thursday night. Family night. Everyone knows what this means. The table will be set at 5pm. The candles will be on. Everything will be tidy and in order. We will sit at the dining table, and eat one of our favourite recipes. We will laugh and discuss, as we always do, the highs and lows, and pits and peaks, of our lives.

On this particular night Dad or Mum will probably bring a thought about of one of our family values, or address a cultural issue within a home that might have gone a little astray. We open it for discussion, and we bring ourselves back to the five values that we agreed on as a family. When the meal is done, the older children get straight into the kitchen to do the dishes, as they do every night. The younger ones clear the table, as the older ones work. Then the little ones will run off and get into their pyjamas after having showers, while the dishes are finished getting done.

When we all reconvene it's usually around the piano or the guitar. Jared starts us all off, and everyone jumps in. It is the most beautiful choir. We will worship in and out of different songs for about 30 minutes to an hour, depending on stamina or the flow in the room. Sometimes one of the children will lead a song that drops into their heart to sing, and we all go in their direction and follow their lead. Between the melodies I can hear one or two praying in tongues, occasionally sharing a prophetic picture that they've seen, or a prayer request.

Everyone has been taught what the etiquette is in that space. In the early days, the little ones were invited to choose that, if they couldn't give their best worship and attention, they would be welcome to go to bed early. The privilege of that special moment, was all the motivation they needed to regulate their postures and their focus, and today those sweet voices are sincere and generous in song.

You might be like me and you don't play an instrument. You might be thinking, I don't know how we would do this as a family. I remember sitting with my four children alone, before we were a household of musicians. A single mother, with her four babes, and making a playlist on the devices that we would roll through, and sing together loud enough to give us confidence to join in, and quiet enough to pray if someone felt prompted. Eventually one of my daughters picked up a guitar and started to learn, and now all four of them play self-taught instruments. They're drawn into it. They aspire towards it, and what a beautiful form of expression they now have.

Worship has become a kind of cultural gift to each of them. In a world that wants to fill their hands with many other things to pick up, worship could probably be a safeguard. Do not allow a lack of musicality to be a determining factor towards worship. The Lord deserves our worship, regardless of our musical ability. The sound of worship should fill our homes, as background music on speakers and playlists, but also as fully-engaged moments of intentional connection as a family, together offering a sacrifice of worship and praise with our own voices.

> *Yet a time is coming and has now come when the true worshipers will worship the Father in the Spirit and in truth, for they are the kind of worshipers the Father seeks. God is spirit, and his worshipers must worship in the Spirit and in truth.*
> *John 4:23-24 (NIV)*

> *"I tell you," he replied, "if they keep quiet, the stones will cry out."*
> *Luke 19:40 (NIV)*

Worship restores order, and transfers authority back to the right place. In reality, the Lord is already established and exalted, far above every other thing. He cannot be lifted any higher than He already is; however what our worship does is correct the perspective *we have* of the way things are.

It determines the spiritual atmosphere. He cannot be magnified any more, but He must be magnified in our eyes. He is already great, but He must be great in our eyes. He is already sovereign, all powerful, and the Lord of lords, but He must take that throne in our hearts as well as in the heavenlies, where He is already established.

When there is any other thing sitting on the throne of our hearts, we are actually in idolatry, unfaithful to Him. Worship puts Him on the throne of our hearts and so we must do this consistently, rhythmically and intentionally; individually, together in our families, and corporately with the Church. Together we enthrone Him, again and again.

For you, Lord, are the Most High over all the Earth;
you are exalted far above all gods.
Psalm 97:9 (NIV)

My worship transfers authority from self or circumstance, into the hands of a sovereign God. My worship returns Him control, and access to the circumstances of my life, in the world around me, in the generation which I live. My worship transfers authority back to where it should be.

When I magnify Him, and honour His name, His dominion is established in my world. When His Name is glorified, everything encapsulated in that Name can be manifest in my reality. When I lift His Name, I release His dominion. This is powerful for our families, Churches, communities, and our cities and nations. We are not singing lyrics with pretty melodies. We are doing warfare. We are accessing the Heavenly realms, and releasing them into our natural realm.

When a family does this, things shift. Breakthroughs begin, and the answers to prayers not even prayed yet, start to become daily bread. The Lord makes self-disclosures in the quiet places we carve out for Him. Those disclosures soothe our souls, calm our nerves, and correct our perspective again. We intentionally choose worship, and praise to correct the posture of our hearts.

When we restore worship in the family unit we are teaching our children the right order of things. We are teaching our children to deny anxiety, by placing worship and honour, reverence and awe, in the face of God. We raise children who become adults, with feet steady on solid foundations, unshaken by the world and the spiritual winds, in the earthquakes so regularly occurring within it.

> *Why, my soul, are you downcast? Why so disturbed within me? Put your hope in God, for I will yet praise Him, my Saviour and my God.*
> *Psalm 42: 1 (NIV)*

The Weapons Of Prayer & Service

We stepped into a new realm of prayer when we blended our two grieving families, and I give credit to Jared for that. His leading foot is always prayer. He aches for spaces and moments alone with the Lord. In the quiet moments of our time with each other, he will often spontaneously break out into praying through a Psalm, or giving thanks, or naming our children, one by one, in prayer.

The last thing I hear every night before drifting off to sleep is him praying over me. Every morning he takes my hand, and prays over my day. When we wrestle through hard topics, he'll interrupt the flow of our (sometimes heated) dialogue with prayer to correct and realign our conversation, and to keep the Lord at the centre.

I have learned so much from Jared about the power of prayer. In response to his leadership in the prayer space for our family, and our Church, and our city, I've seen the Lord's hand in many evident ways. There is no doubt in my heart that prayer is the secret weapon in the arsenal of the believer. I have seen it powerfully at work.

Prayer has become the leading foot of our Church community. We gather together at numerous prayer meetings throughout the week. Those meetings continue to grow. The community comes to adore, intercede, and petition.

All seven of our children are swept up in this current of miracle-releasing prayer. My son, Judah, sees vividly in the spirit realm, and regularly tells me what he can see taking place in our prayer meetings and in our worship. The three older girls sometimes lead in the worship spaces, and release prophetic songs during prayer. Our youngest son, Jesse, regularly has a Scripture, or a prophetic word, to release in prayer meetings, and the little ones are growing in their hearts to worship and pray more, and more, with every passing week.

We have been woven for worship, and given the weapon of prayer. Both are precious forms of communion with the Lord, that will be taught best at the altar of family, before they take on any authentic power in public arenas.

> *Now therefore fear the LORD and serve him in sincerity and in faithfulness. Put away the gods that your fathers served beyond the River and in Egypt, and serve the LORD. And if it is evil in your eyes to serve the LORD, choose this day whom you will serve, whether the gods your fathers served in the region beyond the River, or the gods of the Amorites in whose land you dwell. But as for me and my house, we will serve the LORD.*
> *Joshua 24:14-15 (ESV)*

Much has already been said in this book about the conviction to serve others. We have explored the importance of raising a generation, who live out the gospel of Christ, rather than a gospel of self. Here, I want to invite us to consider a posture of serving the Lord, His house, and His people, not for personal gain but simply because it is the right thing to do. In choosing this path, we are intentionally laying aside the priorities of the world, and embracing the values of Heaven. We are forged for faithfulness.

Throughout Scripture, the Lord uses a single measure for every king and every person: faithfulness. In the end, when we stand before Him, the measure will simply be for good and faithful service. The kings of Israel and Judah were assessed by this same standard. Time and again, their lives are summarized by one question – did they do what was right, or what was evil, in the eyes of the Lord? In the same way, we are called to serve Him as a priority, above all other ventures. One day we will be measured by this alone, the day when it truly matters.

> *And I saw the dead, great and small, standing before the throne, and books were opened. Then another book was opened, which is the book of life. And the dead were judged by what was written in the books, according to what they had done.*
>
> *Revelation 20:12 (ESV)*

My challenge to families is simple. Make weekly Church attendance a priority, and seek a place within your Church community where you can serve actively, meaningfully, and sacrificially. Live out the Great Commission through your own life. How are you making disciples? How are you building the Church, Christ's Body, and Bride? If you are not yet engaged in this, start this week, and commit to doing it faithfully for the rest of your life.

SEASONS IN HOLY CADENCE

If God was in control of your time, how would He have you spend it? Your diary, your schedule, your calendar, your rhythms and patterns, the places you invest your time and your energy – how would that all change if He was calling the shots? How would your calendar change if it was to reflect Biblical principles, Spiritual disciplines, and Kingdom priorities? What would a day look like? What would a week look like? A month? A year?

There's a well-known analogy that is used when describing how to structure our lives around our priorities. It's the analogy of a jar, with a capacity to hold a certain volume of contents. Beside the jar are three mounds – a pile of rocks, a pile of smaller stones, and a pile of sand. All of these items are to fit inside that one jar. If I were to put the sand and the smaller stones in first, I would never be able to fit the big stones. However, if I put the big stones in first, followed by the smaller stones which would fall in and around the big ones, followed by the sand which then fills up every spare space, I would find that all the contents efficiently fitted inside the jar.

Of course, the meaning of this analogy tells us that we must order our lives according to big rocks first. The big rocks represent our priorities; everything else falls in around those priorities in relative order of importance. However, if we allow the urgent and unimportant things to go into our lives first, then our priorities will always be crowded out. Those urgent things scream for our attention, but are rarely the most valuable uses of our time.

So we ask again – what would our week look like if we put Heaven's principles and priorities first? If we denied the urgent and unimportant, for just a moment, to recalibrate our time according to what was most important? What would we do?

What would your week look like if you prioritised your time in the Scriptures and in prayer? What would your week look like if you prioritised the Sabbath rest? What would your week look like if you prioritised the critical family moments that you will never have the second chance to relive over again? What if we truly realised that, this one and only life we have, is a precious treasure trusted to us by the Lord? What if we realised that this life was not a dress rehearsal, that we will never get to do it over again? What if we realised that the potent potential of Heaven lies locked up on the inside of us, and our families, to be stewarded to fruition with all diligence and sobriety? What would my day, week, month, and year look like if I were to live with that keen sense of purpose and stewardship guiding my decisions?

The Lord did not leave us to our own devices to figure it out by trial and error. He was abundantly kind, and abundantly clear, in what our rhythms should look like, for the flourishing and fruition of our potential. The Scriptures tutor us. We are to take daily moments of pause and worship with our Father and our Creator. We are to take one day a week as a Sabbath with Him, in communion, and rest, and worship. We are to take regular holidays and breaks intentionally, as a priority with our families. We are also to take long-term breaks, where the proverbial *field* of our lives can lay fallow to recuperate for future ongoing productivity and health.

I once heard it said that we are to take an hour a day, a day a week, and a week a year, as Sabbath alone with Him. These Sabbath times do not include our family holidays; those are a different type of celebration which are just as important, but a Sabbath is our time of communion and worship, alone with the Lord.

Many years ago I had the privilege of meeting an extraordinary Godly businessman. I managed to steal a few moments to speak with him in between his sessions at a convention. He was a man of great influence, burning with Kingdom purpose, and his eyes shone with a passion so bright that I almost felt I should look away.

During one of his talks, he shared about his practice of setting aside a full day each week to spend in prayer and strategy with the Lord. He described this as his weekly Sabbath, a retreat to his personal wilderness space, completely offline, and out of reach of data or distraction. From sunrise to sunset, every week without fail, he devoted that day solely to communion with God, seeking His direction.

I understood the scale of the work he was doing, and I was amazed that he could find the time to dedicate a full day each week to it. As we stood on the side of the stage, I asked him about it. His response was disarmingly simple. "The work I believe the Lord has given me is far too important for me to carry out in my own strength. This one day each week is the source of all that I do."

Oh, the ache that opened in my spirit as I grasped the weight of that spiritual truth. Since that moment, I have carried this principle with me, applying it in encounters with mighty men and women of God, across political, corporate, and ministry spheres.

> *Isolation comes from a poverty of self; solitude comes from a wealth of self.*
> *Gary Thomas*

Sitting with Christian politicians, in a culture where their colleagues and constituents expect them to work seven days a week, 12 months a year, year after year, I remind them how desperately their constituents need them to be hearing from the Lord. I remind them that they are there in those positions by the Hand of God, to do His bidding and not their own. That they are there to do what is right in the Lord's eyes not what is right in their eyes. The reality is that if the enemy can't make us sin, he will make us distracted, and the more impactful our lives become the greater the tendency to be distracted away from the rhythms required in order to stay connected to the Vine that is Jesus, and the Source which is the Spirit of God.

We must be intentional, extravagant and compelled by priority. We must include others in our modes of rhythms, holidays, and milestones, but also in encouraging them to prioritise in the same way for their own lives. One particular politician went away from our meeting and initiated a compulsory Sabbath for all their office staff. This was a practice that would be unheard of in the political sphere, and yet how transformative this practice would be.

Jesus told us that the Kingdom of God is like yeast that goes through the whole dough and, so when we influence our culture in these seemingly small ways, we are turning culture around. It may be small to begin with, but reformation is the result. The mandate of the Kingdom is Heaven here now – cultural reformation – at the hands of the sons and daughters of God.

> *Jesus also used this illustration: "The Kingdom of Heaven is like the yeast a woman used in making bread. Even though she put only a little yeast in three measures of flour, it permeated every part of the dough."*
> *Matthew 13:33 (NLT)*

> *In this manner, therefore, pray:*
> *Our Father in Heaven,*
> *Hallowed be Your name.*
> *Your Kingdom come.*
> *Your will be done*
> *On Earth as it is in Heaven.*
> *Matthew 6:9-10 (NKJV)*

In our home, there are no other meetings to be at on family night, at times the necessary polite decline is given to invitations which pose to interrupt our family night. From late afternoon, the house begins to fill up, one-by-one, as people return from the activities of their day at work places, university, and school. A special meal is made. Meal time discussion is extended. Board games and card games come out, and we gather around the piano for worship and prayer. At times my eyes have filled with tears, and I've recorded audio voice memos as the choir of voices sings prophetically, and flows together.

It often feels like a whirlpool in the spirit realm, as the worship atmosphere of our hearts, and our home, moves together in the current. Different ones spontaneously lead a new chorus; others share a prophetic picture, or a burden to pray. Family fasts have been prompted, and agreed on, in these nights. Burdens for prayer have vulnerably been shared and carried on behalf of each other. It is not unusual for a breakthrough answer to prayer to greet us the very next morning.

Jared and I Sabbath together every Friday. We slow down, and invest into our marriage. We dream together. We explore the heart of God for the destiny of our family, and all the things that the Lord has called us to. We guard this time every week. There is no shortage of demands that will try to encroach on family time, and on Sabbath, but we have prioritised the rocks in the jar of our lives. The other things can fall in around them, not before them.

> *Hurry is not just a disordered schedule. Hurry is a disordered heart.*
> *John Ortberg*

These are the quiet places of stillness where we pull away from the screaming, roaring demands of the world. We detach ourselves from the pace of keeping up with everybody else. The Hebrew word Sabbath literally means 'to stop'. From the very beginning, God modelled this for humanity. Genesis 2:1-3 tells us that, after creating the heavens and the Earth, God rested on the seventh day, blessed it, and made it holy. Though God does not grow weary, He established a rhythm for humanity; one of rest, completion, and abiding in His presence.

Sabbath is more than a pause from work; it is a day set apart for communion with God. John Mark Comer observes that productivity often declines after about fifty hours of work per week, reflecting the wisdom of six days of labour followed by a day of rest. True rest is intentional and cultivated through connection with God. While sin disrupted humanity's access to this rest, through Jesus, and abiding in His finished work, we can re-enter it.

Sabbath is not simply a day on the calendar – it is a spirit of restfulness that can shape your whole week. John 15 reminds us that a branch cannot bear fruit unless it remains connected to the vine. Likewise, lasting spiritual fruit flows only through abiding in Christ. Sabbath is a reminder to stop, to abide, and to bear fruit through connection, rather than ambition.

The Sabbath is God's. When God declares something holy, He sets it apart for Himself. Observing Sabbath allows us to experience Him, dwell in His presence, and find renewal in a world that constantly demands our attention.

It is a day to stop long enough to:

- Abide in God's presence
- Commune with Him without distraction
- Reflect on His finished work
- Refresh spiritually, emotionally, and mentally

We have learned that the Lord steps into those spaces. What we would find the tendency to strive towards is satisfied, and provided for supernaturally by the Lord, in ways that far exceed any effort we could have invested on our own. To prioritise rest and celebration is an expression of trust in the Lord's provision. We say to our circumstances, and to our hurried souls, "The most important thing to do right now is to be still." In my stillness I trust the Lord's Hand to do a work far greater than I could ever do in my own strength.

Our annual family holidays are booked 12 months in advance, and paced throughout the year, to provide rhythms of rest and celebration. Those holiday retreats hold simple traditions that everyone looks forward to as markers each year. It has blessed me over the years to hear that the older ones still yearn for those simple traditions each year. Traditions, that were initiated when they were just small, still hold their hearts as they mature.

Family rhythms and traditions create identity. They communicate value and priority. They say to a child, "You are the most important thing in the next year's calendar. So important that I've put time with you into the calendar before anything else."

Traditions communicate belonging and identity – quirky, simple things. It might be the location that is frequented every year. It might be a family meal tradition that is reserved for family holidays. It might be a specific board game routine. Whatever it is, tradition and rhythm fortify hearts. Tradition and rhythm serve as an anchor and a reference point. Without them we are tossed by every demand, every circumstance, every challenge, every high, and every low. Without them, we are vulnerable to the schemes of the enemy which ensnare us, deceive us, and lure us away from the strength and purposes in God.

So we return to the question. What would my day, week, month, and year look like if I were to put my priorities into the schedule first? What would my prayer life look like? How would I Sabbath? How would I rest and celebrate? How would I bring my family on the journey as an absolute priority? What if I put my diary on the altar of the family before the Lord? What might it look like then?

SECTION FIVE

Seed & Cities

THE COSMIC CONVERSATION

We don't think enough about legacy. Beyond the here and now; beyond the short term. The way society, and culture, and economics, has been structured over the last number of decades has meant that individuals and households are living week-to-week, and pay cheque to pay cheque, at very best.

Our lives are completely owned – by bosses and rosters, by banks, mortgages, credit card debts, and life-long interest payments. All of us are working tirelessly, just to make ends meet. As a people, we have been turned into desperate consumers, at the mercy of others. A far cry from the Scriptural model for the people of God.

Legacy is woven into the fabric of Heaven's generational economy – the true riches Jesus spoke of (Luke 16:11). Legacy is an essential tenet of Kingdom culture. The clarion call of Yahweh is a generational one. Legacy, heritage, inheritance, and portion. We are to pass down wealth, in every sense, from generation to generation.

> *A good man leaves an inheritance to his children's children,*
> *But the wealth of the sinner is stored up for the righteous.*
> *Proverbs 13:22 (NKJV)*

> *Let each generation tell its children of Your mighty acts;*
> *let them proclaim Your power.*
> *Psalm 145:4 (NLT)*

Our personal vision must extend beyond our own lifetime, and even beyond the lifetimes of our children. Our vision should extend beyond the next 100 years. The contribution I make is one that outlives me, and perpetuates into future generations who I likely will never see with my own eyes.

The wisdom of Proverbs teaches us how. The strength of the patriarchs and matriarchs of Scripture model what is possible in the hands of surrendered lives, and obedient hands. Just ordinary, yet obedient, people with an extraordinary, limitless God. I am absolutely convinced that, unless your conversation with the Lord includes multiple generations after you, He is not interested. The tenets of Scripture have never entertained instant or self-gratification.

HOUSEHOLD DREAMS, KINGDOM PLANS

While many of us are concerned with our own households, the Lord is interested in nations. Abraham wanted a son. The Lord a nation. Hannah wanted a child. The Lord wanted a national leader. It wasn't until that desperate confession and heart desire moved beyond themselves, that the Lord granted them their request. Are you big enough for the Lord to bless you?

> *After these things the word of the Lord came to Abram in a vision, saying, "Do not be afraid, Abram. I am your shield, your exceedingly great reward."*
>
> *But Abram said, "Lord God, what will You give me, seeing I go childless, and the heir of my house is Eliezer of Damascus?" Then Abram said, "Look, You have given me no offspring; indeed one born in my house is my heir!"*
>
> *And behold, the word of the Lord came to him, saying, "This one shall not be your heir, but one who will come from your own body shall be your heir." Then He brought him outside and said, "Look now toward Heaven, and count the stars if you are able to number them." And He said to him, "So shall your descendants be."*
>
> *Genesis 15:1-5 (NKJV)*

Abram (who became Abraham) was being promised a blessing but, in that moment, he could not conceive the fullness of what was being spoken to him. He immediately started talking about not having a successor. The range of view he had was far shorter than what the Lord was talking about. He was thinking merely about his own household. The Lord had something much greater in mind.

I have seen, time and time again, in my own life and in the lives of people around me, that our mindsets are far too small. Our fears, our inadequacies, and the demands that scream for our attention, they all shrink us. We don't see the magnitude of what is in the heart of God. We do not trust or understand His ability to bring it to pass.

Like with Abraham, God knows you are not going to live long enough to spend all that you have coming from Him. So, if we don't start thinking generationally, the cosmic conversation is over.

Our children are the hope of the Kingdom, here and now and into the future. What we leave *to them* is far less important than what we leave *in them*, although both are important. Your mandate, and mine, is to set up future Godly generations in every possible way. Because God's children, the Church, is the hope of the world.

To ask the Lord for provision, to meet only our needs, is far too small a request. Selfish even. My life alone is not big enough to contain the blessing that the Lord wants to pour through me if I were fully available to Him. We are conduits. Vessels. Channels. Access points and portals for Him to move through. We need to start thinking bigger. We need to read the Scriptures, and understand who the children of God truly are intended to be in the Earth.

> *For [even the whole] creation (all nature) waits expectantly and longs earnestly for God's sons to be made known [waits for the revealing, the disclosing of their sonship].*
>
> *Romans 8:19 (AMPC)*

There is greatness inside of you. Bigger, greater and more influential than you realise. The potential cradled on the inside of you is the seed of Heaven. And Heaven never does anything on a mediocre scale. We are holy incubators of the things of God. Waymakers and legacy keepers. The seed in you is a threat to the forces of darkness and, as a result, it suffers resistance. We have to resist the resistance.

For one of my birthdays, a group of girlfriends surprised me with a skydiving ticket. I have to be honest and tell you I am an adrenaline junkie. I was so excited. We woke before dawn that morning, and drove out to a less than impressive office space. It was just around the corner from a small airfield, a few blocks back from the beach. Once we arrived, we spent a little bit of time learning the safety procedures and emergency responses, should they be required. We strapped on our harnesses, and got into the small, rickety plane. Sitting on one of the benches that ran along either side of the cabin, I immediately noticed the silver and black electrical tape on several parts of the plane, and hoped that we were not depending on that tape for the plane to be held together.

Slowly the small plane made its way into the sky, and I had a sudden and overwhelming urge. "Out of this group, I just have to be the one who jumps first," I thought. "If I watch anyone jump out before me, I'll probably change my mind, and refuse to do the jump." I looked into the frightened faces of everyone else in the cabin, and requested they let me go first. They unanimously and eagerly obliged.

As my tandem instructor prepared us both for the jump, he whispered one last thing in my ear. "You have to scream really loud as you're falling. The violence of the opposing velocity of air will take your breath away if you don't force it out of your lungs with all the force you have." And out we went.

Freefalling. Every single one of my senses was completely assaulted. My eyes were watering, my face was being pushed back, and I certainly did push as much air out of my lungs as I could. Falling, falling, falling. Until suddenly the parachute opened and I was surrounded by calm.

Have you ever had to resist the resistance? Have you ever stood in the face of life with all the resolve you could muster? Have you momentarily had your breath taken away, only to quickly realise that your only means of survival is to push back?

The resistance we face in life, in the spirit, in our generation, is not really about us. The enemy is not actually fighting you; he's fighting what is in you. He's trying to sabotage what will come through you. Because if he can get to you, he stops your seed, and he has won. We must resist the resistance.

And I will put enmity (open hostility)
Between you and the woman,
And between your seed (offspring) and her Seed;
He shall [fatally] bruise your head,
And you shall [only] bruise His heel.
Genesis 3:15 (AMP)

The enemy has hated each generation, because of the seed that comes through us. The seed in you is the seed of future generations. The enemy is constantly fighting the *people inside the people*. There are deliverers coming through you. Leaders. Prophets. Kings. He is always after our seed, because this is a generational conversation. The enemy knows that when you get free from your bondage, all those around you are going to be impacted. Your seed was destined in Eden to do damage to darkness.

The enemy knows that the moment you become free marks the end of an old order, and the start of the new. He knows that you will be the start of a new blood line, of kings and priests, victorious and influential.

Addictions – broken. Generational curses – broken. Poverty – broken. Abuse – broken. Lust – broken. Generations of divorce – broken. Hereditary disease, patterns, and bondages – all broken in Jesus' Name!

The enemy knows the world will shift when you get free. He knows that your seed will bruise his head. He knows your children will be free, and that their children will be free, and that each new generation will be stronger than the last. When the wonderful news of the gospel truly touches your life, it turns outward and touches anyone, and everyone, around you.

Choices That Change

I can do all things [which He has called me to do] through Him who strengthens and empowers me [to fulfill His purpose—I am self-sufficient in Christ's sufficiency; I am ready for anything and equal to anything through Him who infuses me with inner strength and confident peace.]
Philippians 4:13 (AMP)

But if the Spirit of Him who raised Jesus from the dead dwells in you, He who raised Christ from the dead will also give life to your mortal bodies through His Spirit who dwells in you.
Romans 8:11 (NKJV)

Your choices are more powerful than generational patterns, or natural limitations. Abraham and Sarah knew what it was like to believe, against all odds, in a promise. Sarah was not physically able to have a child anymore. They were one 100 years old, and 90 years old, respectively. They had no children. And they had waited 25 years between the promise, and the fulfilment of the promise. They even took things into their own hands, believing that, perhaps, Abraham should have an heir through Sarah's servant, Hagar (Genesis 16).

They were dealing with impossible natural conditions. The promise of God was shrouded by impossible circumstances. But we must recognise that the power of the seed within is supernatural, and not something we can ever receive credit for. We are simply stewards of the divine intention of

Heaven coming through us here on Earth. We are to live lives of complete surrender and obedience. This way we recognise the seed of Heaven, and the influence of the Kingdom within each of us.

The Lord will wait till you are humble enough to surrender your life as a vessel for His plans. While you act like you have to make it happen, He is happy to wait. While you are running around, trying to control every outcome, He is happy to wait. While you are gripped with fear over the circumstances, He is happy to wait. While you are reacting out of panic in the opposition, He is happy to wait. He will wait, knowing your limitations, and your circumstances, are no hindrances to His plan.

At the age of 90, Sarah became pregnant. God made her able to do the thing she was not able to do, and He waited till the circumstances were the least favourable. He renamed her from Sarai to Sarah, elevating her position among humanity. And made her the able vessel He always intended her to be.

When the enemy tries to limit us in our circumstances, God makes us able. When the enemy sends adversity, God causes us to rise above. That seed is not threatened by circumstance, because it is a supernatural seed. When we fast forward 42 generations beyond Sarah and Abraham, we meet Jesus. The seed of Abraham. The one who fatally bruised the enemy's head.

> *Now to Abraham and his Seed were the promises made. He does not say, "And to seeds," as of many, but as of one, "And to your Seed," who is Christ.*
> *Galatians 3:16 (NKJV)*

There is a fight going on, because the seed of the righteous brings breakthrough to the generations. God is a God who overrides circumstances. He also increases our capacity. Sometimes the circumstances can be just right, but our thinking is too small.

Let us turn to Hannah for another example. Hannah was loved, and she was a worshipper, but her capacity was too small. Her desires did not move Heaven. They were too small.

> *Now there was a certain man of Ramathaim Zophim, of the mountains of Ephraim, and his name was Elkanah the son of Jeroham, the son of Elihu, the son of Tohu, the son of Zuph, an Ephraimite. And he had two wives: the name of one was Hannah, and the name of the other Peninnah. Peninnah had children, but Hannah had no children. This man went up from his city yearly to worship and sacrifice to the LORD of hosts in Shiloh. Also the two sons of Eli, Hophni and Phinehas, the priests of the LORD, were there. And whenever the time came for Elkanah to make an offering, he would give portions to Peninnah his wife and to all her sons and daughters. But to Hannah he would give a double portion, for he loved Hannah, although the LORD had closed her womb. And her rival also provoked her severely, to make her miserable, because the LORD had closed her womb. So it was, year by year, when she went up to the house of the LORD, that she provoked her; therefore she wept and did not eat.*
> *1 Samuel 1: 1-7 (NKJV)*

Hannah was distraught. Not only did she suffer the grief of barrenness, but she ached under the burdens of mockery and rivalry as well. She suffered with deep injustice. Longing through pain, year after painful year. She looked into her own immediate household, and that was as far as she could see. She wanted a son, but God wanted a national leader.

Friend, almost anyone can birth a son, but it is God who births kings. Almost anyone can build a house, but it is God who builds nations. It was only when Hannah's prayer changed *from introspect to influence* that God's heart was moved.

> *Crushed in soul, Hannah prayed to God and cried and cried – inconsolably.*
> *Then she made a vow:*
> *Oh, God-of-the-Angel-Armies,*
> *If You'll take a good, hard look at my pain,*
> *If You'll quit neglecting me and go into action for me*
> *By giving me a son,*
> *I'll give him completely, unreservedly to You.*
> *I'll set him apart for a life of holy discipline.*
> *1 Samuel 1: 9-11 (MSG)*

We must all take a look deep inside our own hearts and motives, and ask ourselves: *Are my dreams too small? Are the dreams I dream my own, or the Lord's?* God wants to enlarge our vision. He wants to enlarge our capacity. He wants us to become conduits of Heaven into a desperate generation.

The Gospel we are charged with, and charged with passing on to each generation beyond us, has been the most civilising force in history. It has redemptive power for entire communities. Throughout history, the Gospel has reformed the politics, education, health and welfare of entire cities, and countries, and generations. We are not called to raise cute, quiet little families behind white picket fences.

This is a message that brings societal change for the better. The family who grasps the potency of their seed is a force to be reckoned with. The family who knows that dynamic nature, and ability to bring change into the world, is a force that intimidates hell itself. The enemy is not really fighting you; he is fighting what is in you. God wants to see nations, and generations, turned around.

This is not about a comfortable retirement plan, or finally being able to tour the country in an RV collecting shells. When you know the power

of what is in you, it will govern every decision you make. When you know what is at stake, you won't settle or pull back.

After Samuel was born to Hannah, she weaned him and committed him to a life of service in the temple. She came back there, year after year, to worship. She would bring the young Samuel a new coat each year as he grew. Eventually Samuel became the greatest and most revered leader, and prophet, the world had seen in a long time. It was Samuel who recognised young David, and anointed him. It was Samuel who counselled and led kings. It was Samuel who maintained the voice of God, in a generation after the voice of the Lord has been silent for many years. He led the nation in obedience to the Lord's direction. The nation was turned around. He bruised the plans of darkness over that nation.

Other times, our dreams are born into a time of conflict that stunts their progress. In Scripture we see multiple genocides against infants, with the dark purpose to wipe out the leaders destined to bring change. At the time of Moses' birth, and Jesus' birth, the pharaoh and kings of those eras were inspired, by the forces of darkness, to mandate great infanticides. The enemy is so intimidated by the potential of the next generation that he will do whatever it takes to snuff it out before it reaches maturity. Today he does it via abortion, and destruction of the family. He knows there are delivers coming. And so we must fight for life. We must defend it at all costs.

In each of these instances in Scripture, we see that the enemy was not ultimately successful – he is a defeated foe, and the deliverers prevailed. In the same way he will not be successful in your life, because it is the God we love and serve who brings the seed into its maturity. You can be confident of this.

> *Being confident of this very thing, that He who has begun a good work in you will complete it until the day of Jesus Christ;*
>
> *Philippians 1:6 (NKJV)*

Moses survived, and delivered a nation. Jesus survived, and delivered all of humanity. Your seed will make it through the conflict. It will reach full maturity. I am declaring this over your life – you will carry your seed into its maturity.

THE HOUSE OF WISDOM

I am inspired by the juxtaposition the book of Proverbs presents to us. I'm grateful for the contradiction of cultures revealed in this incredible book of Scripture. The contrast between the culture of the world, and the culture of the Kingdom of God, presented with the undercurrent of influence into communities, generations and nations. The book of Proverbs contains keys for living, thriving, and family.

Chapter nine is a beautiful contrast between a godly home, and a worldly home. Two characters are depicted in that chapter. Their names are Wisdom and Folly. They both lead homes, but with opposing motivations and outcomes. Let us consider the urgency and potency line-by-line.

Wisdom has built her house;
she has carved its seven columns.

She has prepared a great banquet,
mixed the wines, and set the table.

She has sent her servants to invite everyone to come.
She calls out from the heights overlooking the city.

"Come in with me," she urges the simple.
To those who lack good judgment, she says,

"Come, eat my food,
and drink the wine I have mixed.

Leave your simple ways behind, and begin to live;
learn to use good judgment."

Anyone who rebukes a mocker will get an insult in return.
Anyone who corrects the wicked will get hurt...

The woman named Folly is brash.
She is ignorant and doesn't know it.

She sits in her doorway
on the heights overlooking the city.

She calls out to men going by
who are minding their own business.

"Come in with me," she urges the simple.
To those who lack good judgment, she says,

"Stolen water is refreshing;
food eaten in secret tastes the best!"

But little do they know that the dead are there.
Her guests are in the depths of the grave.
Proverbs 9:1-6, 13-18 (NLT)

We see here two voices calling out from the same heights. Both promise satisfaction. Only one leads to life. The other leads to the grave.

Nature & Character

Wisdom's character is dignified, constructive, and purposeful. She is calm, constructive, and grounded in truth. The tone of her life is gentle and gracious. We know from the book of Proverbs, all the way through, that she is absolutely lovely.

On the other hand, Folly is loud and brash and ignorant. Her behaviour is obnoxious and cringeworthy.

Preparation

Wisdom builds. And when she builds, she builds beautiful things, lasting things. She is well prepared, stable, and thorough. She has given great thought to the environment she intends to create. When she does her work, she does it with excellence, and to completion. The setting she creates is a solid house with a carefully built banquet hall – a place of generosity and hospitality.

Folly sits in her doorway – a place of idleness and exposure. She is unprepared, and lacks intentionality. The food she offers is cheap, fast, and stolen. Some writers have suggested that the nature of this food speaks of offerings that should have been taken to the temple, but were withheld for personal consumption.

Activity

Wisdom is an industrious leader. She builds, prepares, mixes wine, and sets the table. She has people in her charge, whether that be children, colleagues, or employees. But we know the industry of her home is inclusive of others. All that she is doing is cause-oriented. She knows the table and setting in the environment she is creating, will open its arms to include other people.

Folly, on the other hand, sits idly, lazily watching the world go by, and calling out haphazardly. Her offers and invitations have no substance. Her intentions are self-serving, willingly leading others astray to her own benefit and temporary gratification.

The Invitation

Wisdom has spent her life sowing into the next generation. She has children, disciples and employees who are all organised, and on mission with her. They understand the purpose of the home that they have created with her. They are clear about the message they will carry. And when the time comes, they are sent into their communities with a personal call. They go into their world, seeking and saving those who are lost. Offering them reprieve and restoration.

Folly is alone. She is impulsive and self-serving. There is no greater cause that she lives for; just her own desires, temptations, and lusts. She has relegated to making cheap remarks at passersby – any helpless victim will serve her desires. While Wisdom lives to create a better world for others, Folly lives for herself, with a complete disregard for the devastating impact she will make on those she touches.

Both call out to the simple, and those who lack good judgement. However, Wisdom offers transformation leading to life. Folly offers deception leading to death.

The Message

Wisdom invites the broken and searching into a place of growth and breakthrough. She offers them the path to life. "Come, eat my food and drink the wine I have prepared. Leave your simple ways and live a life you never knew existed." Food has always represented the Word and salvation in the Scriptures, and wine represents the blessing and joy of the Lord. What a beautiful invitation. What a beautiful provision. "Come, be rescued, fed, and richly blessed in this new way of life."

Folly, on the other hand, addresses whoever may be passing her by. There is nothing of hospitality or generosity in her offer. She has nothing of substance to offer, only that which is stolen and fleeting. The invitation is for indulgence and secrecy – illegitimate pleasure void of nourishment.

"Come, stolen water is sweet; food eaten in secret is tasty." Her tone is seductive, reckless, and destructive.

The Outcome

Those who go into Wisdom's house, accepting her invitation, will begin to live and learn good judgement. They will find life and discernment. All those who enter Folly's home are helplessly unaware of the devastation that awaits them.

One home represents God's truth, understanding, and the way of life. The other represents sin, ignorance, and the way of death. Wisdom's house is one of multi-generational legacy. It is established in the community as a place of resource and strength.

These are the homes we build for a legacy that will reach beyond the second and third generation. These are homes where the narrative of transformation is being written, and cultural reformation is ignited.

LIVING SPRINGS

Our homes are temples. Our tables are altars. We must recognise the spiritual significance of these spaces that the Lord has asked us to lead and steward. We simply must think bigger. We must care for more than a white picket fence, and a comfortable existence where our children 'just make it through' to adult lives of mediocre existence. We cannot be satisfied with the status quo, or the lot in life that our world wants to divvy out to us. There is more, my friend. Rise up and create legacy.

In Joshua chapter 15 we read about a remarkable woman known as Caleb's daughter, Achsah (pronounced Ax-ah). The chances are you have never heard a message preached about her, but this woman takes my breath away.

Firstly, we have to understand the context of her family of origin.

You may have heard sermons about Caleb and Joshua, the two men among the twelve spies who explored the Promised Land, and returned with a favourable report. While the other ten spies spread fear and doubt among the Hebrew people, Caleb and Joshua encouraged the nation to trust God, and act in obedience to His promise. They acknowledged the giants in the land, yet their conviction was clear – if the Lord had promised it as their inheritance, faithfulness and obedience were the proper response. They viewed the giants, not as evidence against God's will, but as obstacles to overcome on the path to the promise.

How often do we reject the guidance of the Lord, and the leading of His Spirit, because we face opposition?

How often do we question God's love and intention for us because we come up against the giant?

Can we be a people who are not precious in the face of challenge and hardship?

Could the presence of giants be indicative of the fact that we might actually be right in the middle of God's will?

Caleb and Joshua were different. They remained firm in their obedience of heart. For forty years, they waited in that wilderness before the whole previous rebellious generation had passed away. They held onto the promise of God. Finally, it was time to enter the land they had scouted out forty years earlier.

Eventually, Caleb said to his friend, Joshua, who was now the leader of the nation in place of Moses, "Give me my mountain!" (Joshua 14:12-15).

Caleb declared with great vigour that he was just as strong now, at the age of 80, as he was back then when he saw it for the first time at the age of 40. Joshua gave him, and his family, the land they had been awaiting all these years.

Joshua was a phenomenal leader. I am in awe of him every time I read the story of the Israelite campaigns of exploits. I have the sense that he was reluctant, or on the meeker side of the personality spectrum. His absolute obedience to the Word of God caused him to rise beyond time and time again. He truly was remarkable. Sadly, the account at the end of his life leaves a deep sorrow in my heart.

> *Now Joshua the son of Nun, the servant of the LORD, died when he was one hundred and ten years old. And they buried him within the border of his inheritance at Timnath Heres, in the mountains of Ephraim, on the north side of Mount Gaash. When all that generation had been gathered to their fathers, another generation arose after them who did not know the LORD nor the work which He had done for Israel.*
>
> *Judges 2:8-10 (NKJV)*

It would seem hopeless, if I had not learned of Caleb's remarkable daughter, Achsah. We read about her in Joshua 15.

> *According to the commandment of the LORD to Joshua, he gave to Caleb the son of Jephunneh a portion among the people of Judah, Kiriath-arba, that is, Hebron (Arba was the father of Anak). And Caleb drove out from there the three sons of Anak… And Caleb said, "He who attacks Kiriath-sepher and captures it, I will give him Achsah my daughter as wife." And Othniel the son of Kenaz, the brother of Caleb, captured it. And he gave him Achsah his daughter as wife. When she came to him, she urged him to ask her father for a field. And she dismounted from her donkey, and Caleb said to her, "What do you want?" She said to him, "Give me a blessing. Since you have given me the land of the Negeb, give me also springs of water." And he gave her the upper springs and the lower springs.*
>
> *Joshua 15:13-19 (ESV)*

It turns out that this young woman became a warrior in her own right, who continued the campaign of Israel in her generation. It is wondrous the way that we learn about her, and her father, in this passage of Scripture.

Caleb drives out the three sons of Anak, who were the giants. Long before shepherd boy David slayed Goliath (1 Samuel 17), we see this man, Caleb, in his 80s, take down three giants in a land that he resolutely believed was his, according to the promise of God. What an incredible man!

He generously made investments into the next generation, in both marriage and dominion. He honoured his daughter in a profoundly countercultural way. He gave her land, and he gave her a warrior for a husband. He modelled courage and faith to his daughter.

I love the tenacity of the woman, Achsah. She urges her new husband to ask her father for more land. On the surface that could seem presumptuous, although we see just shortly after the motivation for her request is far greater than comfort for self.

She had a sense of urgency about her, which I admire. She couldn't wait for the proper order of things to play out. She jumped off her donkey ahead of her husband, and made the request herself, a bold move for a woman in a patriarchal society. It makes me laugh to myself, as I often find myself in those awkward situations.

> *And she dismounted from her donkey, and Caleb said to her, "What do you want?" She said to him, "Give me a blessing. Since you have given me the land of the Negeb, give me also springs of water." And he gave her the upper springs and the lower springs.*
> *Joshua 15: 18-19 (ESV)*

She had already been given a beautiful land in the region of Negeb, but her heart desired more. She wanted springs. Springs in Scripture represent a source of life, and often serve as metaphors for encounters with the miraculous and divine. This woman was not happy with her little lot in life – a block of land, and a comfortable dwelling. She wanted springs. She wanted her life to be a place of resource and refreshing to the community she lived in. She wanted to be a place of life-giving springs.

This needs to be the deep longing of our hearts towards our Father. Our requests before him would not be just to meet our own needs. Our request before him should be that He could make us places of refreshing for others. We must think bigger than ourselves, and our needs. But the beauty of Achsah's request doesn't end there. She specifically asked for both the upper and lower springs. Come with me now, friend, into the deep revelation that the Spirit gave me.

The roles of refreshing we carry in our communities, and to our generation, are not only to be a source of life and encounter, but that those encounters happen at both the upper and lower springs. Let me explain.

If society is a river, the lower springs can be seen as places downstream. Where we clothe the naked, feed the hungry, and bind up the broken-hearted. This is the compassionate response of every follower of Jesus. This is our mandate. We are called to care and provide for those in need.

However, you and I are also called to become a generation of people who own the upper springs as well. Upstream – places of policy making, and cultural reformation. Achsah's cry was clear. "Help me serve in culture upstream, as well as nourishing the broken downstream. Help me figure out upstream what's causing the fallout downstream, and help me make an impact there too. While I bind up the broken, help me figure out what is causing the injury, so I can prevent it from happening at all."

Every generation has seen the societal impact of the Kingdom of God. It is the Church who has built schools, universities, and hospitals. The reformers of society have been followers of Jesus. Upper spring impact, with lower spring cleansing. These are the generations we are called to raise. This is the legacy we are called to leave behind.

This is my prophetic word over you, my friend. Your seed is destined to bruise the enemy's head. The temple you create in your home, the altar you build at your table, will bring about mighty men and women in their day and in their hour. They will do great exploits for the King above all Kings, bringing His Kingdom here now, on Earth, as it is in Heaven.

As long as you stay submitted to God's Word. As long as you continue to follow the prompting and empowerment of the Spirit. As long as you continue to resist the resistance, and live a life that is morally obligated to Scripture, and raise your homes accordingly.

Each generation has the potential to be stronger than the last. Some families already have the beautiful benefits of godly heritage in the generations behind them, but not all do. For many of us, this is the envy of our lives, knowing that the patterns we have to break, with intentionality and conviction, are battles that not all have had to fight. It may have to start with you. Or perhaps your call is to steward and perpetuate the gift of Godly legacy you have received.

It is up to all of us to fight, and cut ground into the future, into the unknown, throwing ourselves headlong into the things of God. Our choices are always more powerful than the curses, and the patterns, we may have inherited, or been groomed with. The victorious power of the Cross means that all curses are broken. The empowerment of the precious Holy Spirit makes all things new.

I've thrown myself headlong into Your arms
I'm celebrating Your rescue.
Psalm 13:5 (MSG)

Where the enemy has had a field day with infertility, abortion, venereal disease, negative doctors reports, and shame, we step into a new day of inheritance in the Lord. May the Lord raise up a generation of marriages and families, where a banner of the Lord flies high. A God who heals. A God who preserves. A God who loves, and calls, and draws near. May the Lord raise, in each generation, people who consecrate themselves until marriage, preserving their triune beings for a time of Kingdom impact, through their own families and marriages, into the generations ahead of them.

THE ENDURING POWER OF THE FAMILY ALTAR

As I sit at our family table, I am reminded that the home is the first, and most sacred, ministry we will ever steward. This book has been a journey through seasons of joy, pain, and discovery, and it is here, in the rhythms of our daily life, that God's principles for family are made tangible.

The Family Altar is not a concept to admire from afar; it is alive in the ordinary moments – in the meals shared, the prayers whispered, the laughter and the tears, the quiet study of Scripture, and the songs that rise together from the hearts of those gathered.

I think back to the days when life felt unbearably uncertain. Those days were heavy, yet they became the foundation of a deeper understanding of God's faithfulness. I watched the Lord meet us in our sorrow, sustain us, and give us glimpses of hope that could not have come any other way. In those moments, I began to see what the altar of the home could truly be – a sanctuary where God's presence transforms ordinary life into holy work, where faith is lived rather than merely taught, and where character and courage are cultivated in the soil of everyday practice.

Later, the story of restoration became tangible in ways I could hardly have imagined. We have built a home where the Word is central, where rhythms of prayer, and worship, are prioritised, and where our children encounter God in tangible ways. Moments when faith is caught, not taught. They are the rhythms that form resilience, identity, and hope.

The Family Altar is practical. It is found in meals shared with intention, in board games and laughter that extend beyond recreation into lessons of patience, joy, and connection. It is found in family nights, where prayer rises spontaneously, prophetic words are shared, and burdens are carried together. It is found in bedtime Scripture readings, in teaching children to meditate on the Word, and in celebrating milestones with a heart of gratitude and worship. It is in these simple, repeated acts, that the home becomes a sanctuary, where Heaven meets Earth, and where children learn to recognize God's voice in the ordinary.

Yet the Family Altar is also a call to courage. In a world that demands our attention, where careers, social life, and endless distractions, pull us away. It is a radical decision to make – family, faith, and obedience central. To model a life of faithfulness before our children. To refuse to outsource spiritual formation to screens, or well-meaning institutions. It is not glamorous or easy, but it is life-giving, and it bears fruit that extends far beyond the walls of the home.

I am convinced that the strength of society begins at the Family Altar. When the home is God-centred, faith is authentic, love is cultivated, and hope is transmitted across generations. Marriages thrive, children grow in identity and character, and communities are strengthened. Families who embrace this calling are not building in vain; they are rebuilding the walls of a generation, one home at a time.

I write this, not as a formula, but as a testimony. To the God who restores, sustains, and blesses. To the power of faithfulness in ordinary moments. To the truth that the rhythms of the home – prayer, worship, study, celebration, and rest – are the blueprint for Kingdom impact. God's principles are true. They endure tragedy, opposition, and uncertainty. They transform ordinary life into sacred legacy.

The Family Altar is the place where eternity intersects with today. It is the first ministry, the foundation of culture, and the sanctuary where God's purposes are formed in the hearts of those who dwell there. Let your home be a place of prayer, worship, study, celebration, and obedience. Let it be a refuge where children see faith lived, where marriages are strengthened, and where God's Kingdom is rehearsed daily. When this happens, the light of Heaven spills into the streets, the lonely find belonging, and the broken glimpse redemption.

This is the invitation. The challenge. The privilege. Build your Family Altar. Guard it, cultivate it, and rejoice in it. Stand firm in God's design. In doing so, you participate in the restoration of generations, the renewal of your community, and the advancement of His Kingdom.

Lord,

In the temple and the tables of our homes, may our family altars usher in a miraculous move of Your Spirit. One generation after another.

Lord, would You do it? Would You lead us in Your ways? Would you bring revival and reformation through us?

Amen.

KAROLINA GRANT

Karolina Grant is a trusted Christian voice rising out of Australia. As an author, preacher, podcaster, blogger and pastor, her ministry carries prophetic clarity and a deep devotion to biblical truth. With a background in media, communications and business, and more than two decades of leadership in the local church, she is a strategic thinker and spiritual architect whose words bring revelation and courage to people in every sphere of society. Her heart's single focus is revival that shapes cultural reformation through the generations.

After the passing of her late husband Sam, Karolina continued to lead the Redcliffe location of Citipointe Church with strength, faith and an unwavering passion for building teams. Today she leads with renewed awe at the goodness and sovereignty of God, alongside her husband Jared. Together they are raising their beautifully blended family of seven children.

Karolina's voice calls believers to conviction, purpose and alignment with the Word of God. Her communicative gift carries both tenderness and fire, leaving audiences strengthened, awakened and equipped for every season.

B.Bus (IntBus) B.A. (Jour)
Website: karolinagrant.com
Instagram: @karolinagrant_

www.ingramcontent.com/pod-product-compliance
Lightning Source LLC
LaVergne TN
LVHW091132080826
845145LV00008B/2125

* 9 7 8 1 7 6 4 4 4 3 0 6 7 *